SADLIER-OXFORD   **LEVEL E**

Vocabulary
Workshop
Enhanced Edition

The classic program for:

- *developing* and *enhancing* vocabulary resources

- *promoting* more effective communication in today's world

- *improving* vocabulary skills assessed on standardized and/or college-admission tests

---

By
Jerome Shostak

Sadlier-Oxford

A Division of William H. Sadlier, Inc.
9 Pine Street
New York, New York 10005-1002
1-800-221-5175

Contents

ISBN: 0-8215-0610-2
10 11 12 13 14/05 04 03 02 01

Foreword

For close to five decades VOCABULARY WORKSHOP has been a highly successful tool for guiding and stimulating systematic vocabulary growth for students. It has also been extremely valuable for preparing students to take the types of standardized vocabulary tests commonly used to assess grade placement, competence for graduation, and/or college readiness. The *Enhanced Edition* has faithfully maintained those features that have made the program so beneficial in these two areas, while introducing new elements to keep abreast of changing times and changing standardized-test procedures, particularly the SAT. The features that make VOCABULARY WORKSHOP so valuable include:

Word List
Each book contains 300 or more basic words, selected on the basis of:
• currency in present-day usage
• frequency on recognized vocabulary lists
• applicability to standardized tests
• current grade-placement research

Units
The words in each book are organized around 15 short, stimulating *Units* featuring:
• pronunciation and parts of speech
New! • definitions—fuller treatment in the *Enhanced Edition*
• synonyms and antonyms
• usage (one phrase and two sentences)

Reviews
Five *Reviews* highlight and reinforce the work of the units through challenging exercises involving:
New! • shades of meaning (SAT-type critical-thinking exercise)
• definitions
• synonyms and antonyms
• analogies
• sentence completions
• word families

Cumulative Reviews
Four *Cumulative Reviews* utilize standardized testing techniques to provide ongoing assessment of word mastery, all involving SAT-type critical-thinking skills. Here the exercises revolve around
New! • shades of meaning   • analogies   • two-word completions

Additional Features
• A *Diagnostic Test* provides ready assessment of student needs at the outset of the term.
• The *Vocabulary of Vocabulary* reviews terms and concepts needed for effective word study.
• The *Final Mastery Test* provides end-of-term assessment of student achievement.
• *Building with Word Roots* introduces the study of etymology.
• *Enhancing Your Vocabulary,* Levels F through H, introduces students to the study of word clusters.
New! • *Working with Parts of Speech,* Levels F through H, provides further work with word clusters and introduces 50 new words per level.

Ancillary Materials
• An *Answer Key* for each level supplies answers to all materials in the student text.
• A *Series Teacher's Guide* provides a thorough overview of the features in each level, along with tips for using them effectively.
• The *Supplementary Testing Program: Cycle One, Cycle Two* provide two complete programs of separate and different testing materials for each level, so testing can be varied. A *Combined Answer Key* for each level is also available.
• The SAT-type *TEST PREP Blackline Masters* for each level provide further testing materials designed to help students prepare for SAT-type standardized tests.
• An *Interactive Audio Pronunciation Program* is also available for each level.

Pronunciation Key

The pronunciation is indicated for every basic word introduced in this book. The symbols used for this purpose, as listed below, are similar to those appearing in most standard dictionaries of recent vintage. The author has consulted a large number of dictionaries for this purpose but has relied primarily on *Webster's Third New International Dictionary* and *The Random House Dictionary of the English Language (Unabridged)*.

There are, of course, many English words for which two (or more) pronunciations are commonly accepted. In virtually all cases where such words occur in this book, the author has sought to make things easier for the student by giving just one pronunciation. The only significant exception occurs when the pronunciation changes in accordance with a shift in the part of speech. Thus we would indicate that *project* in the verb form is pronounced prə 'jekt, and in the noun form, 'präj ekt.

It is believed that these relatively simple pronunciation guides will be readily usable by the student. It should be emphasized, however, that the *best* way to learn the pronunciation of a word is to listen to and imitate an educated speaker.

Vowels

ā	lake	e	stress	ü	loot, new
a	mat	ī	knife	u̇	foot, pull
â	care	i	sit	ə	rug, broken
ä	bark, bottle	ō	flow	ər	bird, better
au̇	doubt	ô	all, cord		
ē	beat, wordy	oi	oil		

Consonants

ch	child, lecture	s	cellar	wh	what
g	give	sh	shun	y	yearn
j	gentle, bridge	th	thank	z	is
ŋ	sing	th̶	those	zh	measure

All other consonants are sounded as in the alphabet.

Stress

The accent mark *precedes* the syllable receiving the major stress: en 'rich

Parts of Speech

adj.	adjective	*int.*	interjection	*prep.*	preposition
adv.	adverb	*n.*	noun	*v.*	verb
		part.	participle		
		pl.	plural		

The Vocabulary of Vocabulary

There are some interesting and useful words which are employed to describe and identify words. The exercises that follow will help you to check and strengthen your knowledge of the "vocabulary of vocabulary."

Synonyms and Antonyms

Synonyms

A *synonym* is a word that is similar in meaning to another word.

EXAMPLES:

eat—consume   clash—conflict
hurt—injure   fire—discharge

Exercises

*In each of the following groups, encircle the word that is most nearly the **synonym** of the first word in **boldface type**.*

1. amuse
a. delight
b. fancy
c. clear
d. deport

2. abundant
a. healthy
b. distant
c. ample
d. clever

3. hidden
a. conquered
b. hated
c. admired
d. concealed

4. craftsman
a. native
b. motorist
c. skilled worker
d. employee

5. melody
a. bar
b. staff
c. violin
d. tune

6. neat
a. sloppy
b. dull
c. tidy
d. overworked

7. continue
a. halt
b. inspect
c. condemn
d. endure

8. influence
a. position
b. money
c. education
d. effect

Antonyms

An *antonym* is a word that is opposite in meaning to another word.

EXAMPLES:

enter—leave   happy—miserable
wild—tame   leader—follower

Exercises

*In each of the following groups, encircle the word that is most nearly the **antonym** of the first word in **boldface type**.*

1. apparent
a. chance
b. risky
c. concealed
d. clear

2. feast
a. order
b. banquet
c. recipe
d. fast

3. fiction
a. ideal
b. truth
c. novel
d. notion

4. fix
a. trouble
b. please
c. change
d. break

5. honest
a. profitable
b. deceitful
c. gentle
d. loud

6. curious
a. odd
b. uninterested
c. neat
d. careful

7. difficult
a. easy
b. forceful
c. stubborn
d. boring

8. visible
a. concerned
b. content
c. possible
d. hidden

Words Pronounced Alike; Words Spelled Alike

Homonyms

A *homonym* is a word having the same pronunciation as another word but a different meaning and a different spelling.

EXAMPLES:

know—no   pale—pail
horse—hoarse   flee—flea

Exercises

*In each of the following sentences, encircle in the parentheses the **homonym** that correctly completes the meaning.*

1. The judge (**fined, find**) the owner of the dog for allowing it to be in the streets without a leash.

2. To me the most beautiful of all (**flowers, flours**) is the early June rose.

3. I felt very uncomfortable being the (**lone, loan**) passenger on the bus.

4. I plan to (**where, wear**) my new outfit to school tomorrow.

5. I still do not know whether it was the (**rite, right, write**) thing to have done.

6. He placed the gift in a (**plane, plain**) box.

7. I watched the aircraft (**soar, sore**) out of sight.

8. I felt as though everyone in the theater was (**staring, stairing**) at me.

9. I think I have (**pored, poured**) some salt into the sugar bowl!

10. It costs more than I could (**urn, earn**) in a month.

Homographs

A *homograph* is a word that has the same spelling as another word but a different meaning.

EXAMPLES:

Spell may mean to indicate the letters of a word.
Spell may mean a charm or incantation.
Spell may mean an interval of rest or inactivity.

Most homographs, like those above, are not only spelled alike but pronounced alike. There are some, however, that are pronounced differently.

EXAMPLES:

Close, meaning to shut, is pronounced *klōz*.
Close, meaning nearby, is pronounced *klōs*.

Tear, meaning to rip, is pronounced *târ*.
Tear, meaning a drop of salty water from the eye, is pronounced *tēr*.

Homographs that are pronounced differently are sometimes called *heteronyms*.

Exercises   *In Column C, write the homograph suggested by the definitions given in Columns A and B. The initial letter of the required word is given and the dashes represent the missing letters.*

Column A	Column B	Column C
1. to declare	country	s _ _ _ _
2. to wear out	outer layer on wheel	t _ _ _
3. Chinese boat	worthless material	j _ _ _
4. place of trial	to woo	c _ _ _ _ _
5. large basket	to hinder	h _ _ _ _ _

Parts of a Word

Prefixes   A *prefix* is a syllable or syllables placed at the beginning of a word.

EXAMPLES: *ex- dis- ab- per- in-*

Suffixes   A *suffix* is a syllable or syllables placed at the end of a word.

EXAMPLES: *-ant -ence -or -ation*

Bases   A *base* or *root* is the main part of the word to which prefixes and suffixes may be added.

EXAMPLES: *-fact- -pend- -sist-*

Combining the prefix *in-* with the base *-sist-* and the suffix *-ence* gives us the word *insistence.*

NOTE: The term *affix* may be used to designate either a prefix or a suffix. An affix is any addition to the base or root of a word.

Exercises   *Divide each of the following words into its prefix, root, and suffix. Some of the words do not have either a prefix or a suffix. The first word has been done for you.*

Word	Prefix	Root	Suffix
1. compartment	**com**	**part**	**ment**
2. resented	_____	_____	_____
3. enacting	_____	_____	_____
4. interruption	_____	_____	_____
5. diction	_____	_____	_____
6. addict	_____	_____	_____
7. recently	_____	_____	_____
8. complicate	_____	_____	_____
9. helpless	_____	_____	_____
10. referral	_____	_____	_____

Denotation and Connotation

Denotation   The denotation of a word is its specific dictionary meaning.

Examples:

Word	Denotation
eminent	noteworthy or distinguished
cumbersome	hard to handle or manage
remember	call to mind

Connotation   The *connotation* of a word is its tone—that is, the emotions or associations it normally arouses in people using, hearing, or reading it. Depending on what these feelings are, the connotation of a word may be *favorable (positive)* or *unfavorable (pejorative)*. A word that does not normally arouse strong feelings of any kind has a *neutral* connotation.

Examples:

Word	Connotation
eminent	favorable
cumbersome	unfavorable
remember	neutral

Exercises   *In the space provided, label the connotation of each of the following words **F** for "favorable," **U** for "unfavorable," or **N** for "neutral."*

_____ **1.** mediocre	_____ **5.** reek	_____ **9.** plan
_____ **2.** article	_____ **6.** intrepid	_____ **10.** liberality
_____ **3.** drudgery	_____ **7.** sudden	_____ **11.** render
_____ **4.** enlightened	_____ **8.** clique	_____ **12.** illustrious

Literal and Figurative Usage

Literal Usage   When a word is used in a *literal* sense, it is being employed in its strict (or primary) dictionary meaning in a situation (or *context*) that "makes sense" from a purely logical point of view.

Example: Yesterday I read an old tale about a knight who slew a *fire-breathing* dragon.

Figurative Usage   Sometimes words are used in a symbolic or nonliteral way in situations that do not "make sense" from a purely logical point of view. We call this nonliteral or "extended" application of a word a *figurative* or *metaphorical* usage.

Example: Suddenly my boss rushed into my office *breathing fire*.

Exercises   *In the space provided, write **L** for "literal" or **F** for "figurative" next to each of the following sentences to show how the italicized expression is being used.*

_____ **1.** Tom *danced* with Sally at the prom.

_____ **2.** All kinds of delightful images *dance* across the pages of that novel.

_____ **3.** When I saw how popular he was with my friends, I turned *green* with envy.

_____ **4.** Last year I bought a new *green* pickup truck.

_____ **5.** It takes a *green* young rookie years to become a seasoned, streetwise veteran.

_____ **6.** The corn was not harvested while it was still *green*.

_____ **7.** As long as we don't have the funds to produce this project, it will have to stay *on the back burner*.

_____ **8.** I left the stew simmering *on the back burner* for several hours.

Analogies

An *analogy* is a comparison. For example, we can draw an analogy, or comparison, between a bird and an airplane.

In an examination, you will be asked to show that you know the meanings of words, and that you can think clearly, by recognizing an analogy between two different pairs. In the most common form of analogy question, two words are given that have a certain relationship. Then you are to select another pair of words having the same relationship.

EXAMPLE:

count is to **calculate** as
a. expand is to contract
b. plead is to annoy
c. turn is to twist
d. tire is to refresh

The relationship between the given pair of words, *calculate* and *count*, is that they are roughly *the same* in meaning. Look at the four other pairs of words. Which of them are most nearly synonyms? The answer clearly is (*c*) "turn is to twist" because *turn* and *twist* have the same essential meaning.

Exercises *In each of the following, encircle the item that best completes the analogy.*

1. peculiar is to **usual** as
a. loud is to musical
b. odd is to ordinary
c. wrong is to incorrect
d. angry is to mad

2. one is to **many** as
a. last is to most
b. cost is to price
c. soldier is to regiment
d. copy is to original

3. increase is to **heighten** as
a. crease is to fold
b. exclude is to include
c. lower is to involve
d. fear is to greet

4. donate is to **accept** as
a. remember is to recall
b. serve is to pay
c. perceive is to notice
d. give is to take

5. clear is to **cloudy** as
a. timid is to fearful
b. small is to tiny
c. bright is to dark
d. fine is to expensive

6. lucky is to **unfortunate** as
a. distant is to far
b. lost is to misplaced
c. found is to lost
d. tired is to weak

7. penniless is to **wealthy** as
a. strong is to muscular
b. dry is to arid
c. cowardly is to brave
d. hungry is to sleepy

8. pear is to **fruit** as
a. apple is to animal
b. cat is to mineral
c. sun is to element
d. pea is to vegetable

9. degree is to **temperature** as
a. pound is to weight
b. ruler is to length
c. ounce is to distance
d. foot is to capacity

10. shed is to **mansion** as
a. office is to mayor
b. eraser is to pencil
c. horse is to deer
d. bicycle is to automobile

Context Clues

When you do the various word-omission exercises in this book, look for *context clues* built into the passage to guide you to the correct answer.

Restatement Clues

A *restatement clue* consists of a synonym for, or a definition of, a missing word.

Example:

"I'm willing to <u>tell</u> you what I know about the matter," the reporter said, "but I can't _____ my sources."

a. conceal   b. defend   c. prosecute   ⓓ reveal

Contrast Clues

A *contrast clue* consists of an antonym for, or a phrase that means the opposite of, a missing word.

Example:

"I'm trying to <u>help</u> you, <u>not</u> (**assist, ⓗhinder**)) you!" I exclaimed in annoyance.

Inference Clues

An *inference clue* implies but does not directly state the meaning of a missing word.

Example:

A <u>utility infielder</u> has to be a very _____ player because he is a veritable "<u>jack-of-all-trades</u>" on the _____ <u>diamond</u>.

ⓐ veteran . . . football   c. experienced . . . hockey
ⓑ versatile . . . baseball   d. energetic . . . golf

Exercises   *Use context clues to choose the word or words that complete each of the following sentences or sets of sentences.*

1. Jonathan Swift once said that he didn't like people as a group but that he could put up with them _____ .

a. collectively   b. mechanically   c. individually   d. compactly

2. "Don't take the _____ off the line yet," mom told me as I searched around for the clothespin bag. "It is still _____ to the touch."

a. laundry . . . damp
b. telephone . . . dull
c. wash . . . dry
d. clothes . . . dirty

3. If you will supply the dishes for the picnic, I will (**furnish, eat**) the food.

Diagnostic Test

This test contains a sampling of the words that are to be found in the exercises in this Vocabulary Workshop. It will give you an idea of the types and levels of the words to be studied. When you have completed all the units, the Final Mastery Test at the end of this book will assess what you have learned. By comparing your results on the Final Mastery Test with your results on the Diagnostic Test below, you will be able to judge your progress.

Synonyms   *In each of the following groups, encircle the word or phrase that most nearly expresses the meaning of the word in* **boldface type** *in the introductory phrase.*

1. an **unkempt** appearance
a. sudden   b. untidy   c. necessary   d. voluntary

2. chemicals that **adulterate** the food
a. consume   b. pollute   c. purify   d. color

3. part of an **insidious** plan
a. treacherous   b. recent   c. awkward   d. logical

4. the **belligerent** nations
a. neighborly   b. wealthy   c. hostile   d. poor

5. lost in the **holocaust**
a. confusion   b. struggle   c. results   d. great fire

6. an **adroit** driver
a. careful   b. experienced   c. skillful   d. careless

7. a **cursory** examination
a. hasty   b. thorough   c. very painful   d. rewarding

8. **delete** a portion of the selection
a. read   b. cross out   c. emphasize   d. misunderstand

9. a clever **artifice**
a. worker   b. reaction   c. statement   d. trick

10. seek **redress**
a. health   b. remedy   c. costume   d. custom

11. **scrupulous** attention to details
a. expert   b. careful   c. slight   d. childish

12. offer as a **panacea**
a. cure-all   b. substitute   c. moneymaker   d. token

13. **cogent** reasoning
a. false   b. organized   c. dulled   d. forceful

14. **altruistic** motives
a. unselfish   b. complex   c. obvious   d. inner

15. **embark** at once
a. cut   b. notice   c. cover   d. board

16. plead for **clemency**
a. justice b. mercy c. understanding d. release

17. accede to their requests
a. listen b. consent c. deny d. alter

18. an **officious** guard
a. efficient b. hired c. powerful d. meddlesome

19. a **musty** closet
a. large b. concealed c. smelly d. locked

20. an **endemic** species
a. interesting b. native c. peculiar d. valuable

21. reprehensible behavior
a. worthy b. blameworthy c. criminal d. remarkable

22. turbulent days
a. violent b. fast c. rainy d. muddy

23. no longer **extant**
a. in existence b. happy c. in prison d. visible

24. a **compatible** couple
a. married b. divorced c. agreeing d. elderly

25. deride our efforts
a. compliment b. mock c. defend d. extend

26. a **stentorian** voice
a. loud b. grating c. high d. hushed

27. gnarled tree trunks
a. damaged b. cut c. knotty d. tall

28. a **poignant** scene
a. humorous b. moving c. tiresome d. noisy

29. copious notes
a. scribbled b. clever c. imitative d. plentiful

30. unable to **acquiesce**
a. go along with b. leave c. obtain d. understand

Antonyms *In each of the following groups, encircle the word or expression that is most nearly **opposite** in meaning to the word in **boldface type** in the introductory phrase.*

31. a worthy **adversary**
a. undertaking b. opponent c. ally d. cause

32. a **dearth** of ideas
a. lack b. association c. source d. abundance

33. venal arrangements
a. workable b. honorable c. corrupt d. helpful

34. an overly **indulgent** parent
a. energetic b. unconcerned c. strict d. confident

35. a **callous** attitude
a. sensitive b. hostile c. surprising d. distant

36. a **quiescent** volcano
a. dormant   b. imposing   c. active   d. small

37. a **loquacious** person
a. tight-lipped   b. openhanded   c. farsighted   d. narrow-minded

38. **perpetuate** a family tradition
a. defend   b. observe   c. discontinue   d. question

39. **retrogress** in ability
a. fall behind   b. advance   c. fail   d. bask

40. the **placid** waters of the lake
a. peaceful   b. agitated   c. polluted   d. sparkling

41. made some very **trenchant** comments
a. revealing   b. strange   c. amusing   d. inane

42. **misconstrue** its meaning
a. question   b. understand   c. dislike   d. enjoy

43. **quell** an armed uprising
a. report   b. instigate   c. join   d. crush

44. a **voluminous** report
a. valuable   b. brief   c. learned   d. written

45. **disparaging** remarks
a. negative   b. unusual   c. tasteless   d. complimentary

46. since the plan appears to be **feasible**
a. uncomplicated   b. innocuous   c. unworkable   d. inexpensive

47. a truly **virulent** strain of the virus
a. unusual   b. mild   c. recent   d. deadly

48. a **suave** young man
a. clever   b. boorish   c. haughty   d. kindly

49. a **meticulous** worker
a. diligent   b. contented   c. retired   d. careless

50. with **negligible** results
a. substantial   b. curious   c. negative   d. unexpected

Unit 1

Definitions   *Note carefully the spelling, pronunciation, and definition of each of the following words. Then write the word in the blank space in the illustrative phrase following.*

1. **adulterate**   (v.) to corrupt, make worse by the addition of something
   (ə 'dəl tə rāt)   of lesser value

   _____ the milk with water

2. **ambidextrous**   (adj.) able to use both hands equally well; very skillful;
   (am bi 'dek strəs)   deceitful, hypocritical

   marveled at his _____ abilities

3. **augment**   (v.) to make larger, increase
   (ôg 'ment)

   _____ one's income

4. **bereft**   (part., adj.) deprived of; made unhappy through a loss
   (bi 'reft)

   _____ of friends in his old age

5. **deploy**   (v.) to position or arrange; to utilize; to form up
   (di 'ploi)

   _____ troops for battle

6. **dour**   (adj.) stern, unyielding; gloomy, ill-humored
   (daůr)

   a _____ and sullen disposition

7. **fortitude**   (n.) courage in facing difficulties
   ('fôr ti tüd)

   showed great _____ during the
   flood

8. **gape**   (v.) to stare with open mouth; to open the mouth wide; to
   (gāp)   open wide

   _____ in wonder at the sight

9. **gibe**   (v.) to utter taunting words; (n.) an expression of scorn
   (jīb)

   _____ at him for his cowardice

10. **guise**   (n.) an external appearance, cover, mask
    (gīz)

    the _____ of a police officer

11. **insidious**   (adj.) intended to deceive or entrap; sly, treacherous
    (in 'sid ē əs)

    an _____ scheme

12. **intimation**   (n.) a hint, indirect suggestion
    (int ə 'mā shən)

    gave no _____ of her difficulties

13. **opulent**   (adj.) wealthy, luxurious; ample; grandiose
    ('äp yə lənt)

    _____ living quarters

14. **pliable**   (adj.) easily bent, flexible; easily influenced
    ('plī ə bəl)

    three spools of _____ copper wire

15. reiterate
(rē 'it ə rāt)

(*v.*) to say again, repeat

_____ a statement for emphasis

16. stolid
('stäl id)

(*adj.*) not easily moved, mentally or emotionally; dull, unresponsive

a _____ person who takes everything in stride

17. tentative
('ten tə tiv)

(*adj.*) experimental in nature; uncertain, hesitant

a _____ arrangement

18. unkempt
(ən 'kempt)

(*adj.*) not combed; untidy; not properly maintained; unpolished, rude

seemed to take pride in being _____

19. verbatim
(vər 'bā təm)

(*adj., adv.*) word for word; exactly as written or spoken

repeat _____

20. warily
('wâr ə lē)

(*adv.*) cautiously, with great care

approach the mouth of the cave _____

**Completing
the Sentence**

From the words for this unit, choose the one that best completes each of the following sentences. Write the word in the space provided.

1. At the risk of being boring, let me _____ my warning against careless driving.

2. In Shakespeare's famous tragedy *Othello*, Iago comes to Othello in the _____ of a friend but proves to be a deadly enemy.

3. Why would someone who is usually so neat and tidy appear in public in such a(n) _____ state?

4. America's earliest settlers faced the hardships of life on the frontier with _____ and faith.

5. Perhaps I would be bored with the _____ lifestyle of a millionaire, but I'm willing to try it.

6. Having learned to respect the power in his opponent's fists, the boxer circled _____ around the center of the ring.

7. The twigs that were to be woven into the basket were soaked in water to make them more _____.

8. How can you tell whether the chopped-meat patty you ate for lunch had been _____ with artificial coloring and other foreign substances?

12

9. We learned that beneath his _____ exterior there was a sensitive, highly subtle and perceptive mind.

10. The company commander called his troops together and asked for more volunteers to _____ the strength of the raiding party.

11. Since I need the speaker's exact words for my report, I have asked the stenographer to take down the speech _____.

12. His unchanging facial features and controlled voice as he received the news gave no _____ of his true feelings.

13. What a tragedy that in the twilight of her life the unfortunate woman should be _____ of all her loved ones!

14. Why should I be the object of all those _____ just because I'm wearing baby-blue Bermuda shorts on campus?

15. Many ballplayers can bat from either side of the plate, but they cannot throw well with each hand unless they are _____.

16. To this day, historians are still debating whether or not Aaron Burr was guilty of a(n) _____ plot to break up the United States.

17. Since his acceptance of the invitation was only _____ , the hostess may be one man short at the dinner party.

18. The _____ expressions on the jurors' faces as they grimly filed back into the courtroom did not bode well for the defendant.

19. As the magician's beautiful blond assistant seemed to vanish into thin air, the entire audience _____ in amazement.

20. An experienced baseball manager _____ his outfielders according to the strengths or weaknesses of the opposing batters.

Synonyms   *From the words for this unit, choose the one that is most nearly **the same** in meaning as each of the following groups of expressions. Write the word on the line given.*

1. rich, lavish; plentiful, abundant   _____

2. to ridicule, mock, deride, jeer   _____

3. carefully, prudently, gingerly   _____

4. to contaminate, pollute, sully   _____

5. impassive, phlegmatic, unresponsive   _____

6. a costume, semblance; a pretense   _____

7. harsh, bleak, forbidding, saturnine   _____

8. provisional, inconclusive   _____

9. cunning, underhanded, perfidious _____

10. word for word, exact _____

11. sloppy, disheveled; disordered; rough _____

12. resolve, steadfastness, mettle _____

13. supple, adaptable, resilient _____

14. a clue, indication, inkling _____

15. to arrange, station, organize _____

16. to gawk, ogle; to open wide _____

17. deprived; saddened by loss, bereaved _____

18. equally skillful with both hands _____

19. to enlarge, supplement, amplify _____

20. to repeat, rehash _____

Antonyms   *From the words for this unit, choose the one that is most nearly* **opposite** *in meaning to each of the following groups of expressions. Write the word on the line given.*

1. poverty-stricken, wretched, destitute _____

2. to decrease, diminish _____

3. cheery, inviting, genial _____

4. fearfulness, timidity, faintheartedness _____

5. rigid, inflexible, recalcitrant _____

6. definite, conclusive, confirmed _____

7. to purify, purge, expurgate _____

8. paraphrased _____

9. emotional, oversensitive; high-strung _____

10. frank, ingenuous, aboveboard _____

11. a compliment, praise _____

12. well-groomed, tidy, neat, natty _____

13. recklessly, heedlessly, incautiously _____

14. clumsy, all thumbs, maladroit _____

15. a direct or blunt communication _____

16. replete, well provided with _____

14

1. Recruits who complain of the cold should try to show a little more intestinal (**fortitude, intimation**) in facing the elements.

2. The young prince, who much preferred blue jeans, had to dress in the (**stolid, opulent**) robes designed for the coronation.

3. Though all hope of victory had faded, the remaining troops continued to resist the enemy with a (**bereft, dour**) tenacity.

4. The speaker (**deployed, adulterated**) all the facts and figures at her command to buttress her argument.

5. I soon found out that my supposed friend had taken it upon himself to repeat (**unkempt, verbatim**) every word I said about Frieda's party.

6. What a bore to hear the same silly advertising slogans (**gaped, reiterated**) endlessly on TV programs!

7. Do you believe that the curriculum will be (**stolid, adulterated**) if courses like driver education and consumer science are introduced?

8. The ticking grew louder as the bomb squad (**warily, pliably**) opened the package found on the grounds of the Governor's residence.

9. Let us not forget that the early fighters for women's rights were greeted with the (**gibes, guise**) of the unthinking mob.

10. What he calls his "(**insidious, pliable**) outlook on life" seems to me simply a lack of any firm moral standards.

11. A sort of heaviness in the air and an eerie silence were the first real (**reiterations, intimations**) of the approaching cyclone.

12. One of the chief reasons for his dateless weekends is undoubtedly his (**opulent, unkempt**) appearance.

13. There we were at the very edge of the cliff, with our front wheels about to plunge into a (**gaping, intimating**) ravine!

14. Do you expect me to listen to a lot of tired old ideas dressed up in the (**fortitude, guise**) of brilliant new insights?

15. In this scene of wild jubilation, my (**stolid, tentative**) roommate continued to eat his peanut butter sandwich as though nothing had happened.

16. Jane must have been (**bereft, pliable**) of her senses when she bought that old car!

17. By studying the reactions of simpler life forms, researchers have greatly (**augmented, adulterated**) our knowledge of human behavior.

18. Because of my inexperience, I did not recognize at first his (**insidious, ambidextrous**) attempts to undermine our employer's confidence in me.

19. Have you heard the joke about the (**ambidextrous, opulent**) loafer who was equally adept at not working with either hand?

20. Because the situation is changing so rapidly, any plans we make to deal with the emergency can be no more than (**verbatim, tentative**).

Unit 2

Definitions

Note carefully the spelling, pronunciation, and definition of each of the following words. Then write the word in the blank space in the illustrative phrase following.

1. adroit
(ə 'droit)

(*adj.*) skillful, expert in the use of the hands or mind

_____ at twirling a rope

2. amicable
('am ə kə bəl)

(*adj.*) peaceable, friendly

an _____ settlement of the dispute

3. averse
(ə 'vərs)

(*adj.*) having a deep-seated distaste; opposed, unwilling

_____ to strenuous exercise

4. belligerent
(bə 'lij ə rənt)

(*adj.*) given to fighting, warlike; combative, aggressive; (*n.*) one at war, one engaged in war

a _____ answer

5. benevolent
(bə 'nev ə lənt)

(*adj.*) kindly, charitable

a _____ feeling toward all their neighbors

6. cursory
('kər sə rē)

(*adj.*) hasty, not thorough

a _____ glance at the document

7. duplicity
(dü 'plis ə tē)

(*n.*) treachery, deceitfulness

fired the employees suspected of _____

8. extol
(ek 'stōl)

(*v.*) to praise extravagantly

_____ her heroic deeds

9. feasible
('fē zə bəl)

(*adj.*) possible, able to be done

develop a _____ plan of action

10. grimace
('grim əs)

(*n.*) a wry face, facial distortion; (*v.*) to make a wry face

a _____ of pain

11. holocaust
('häl ə kôst)

(*n.*) a large-scale destruction, especially by fire; a vast slaughter; a burnt offering

a victim of the Chicago _____

12. impervious
(im 'pər vē əs)

(*adj.*) not affected or hurt by; admitting of no passage or entrance

a plastic cover _____ to moisture

13. impetus
('im pə təs)

(*n.*) a moving force, impulse, stimulus

gave a new _____ to the drive

14. jeopardy
('jep ər dē)

(*n.*) danger

mistakes that put the entire operation in serious

_____

15. meticulous
(mə 'tik yə ləs)

(*adj.*) extremely careful; particular about details

a _____ housekeeper

16. nostalgia
(nä 'stal jə)

(*n.*) a longing for something past; homesickness

a vague feeling of _____

17. quintessence
(kwin 'tes əns)

(*n.*) the purest essence or form of something; the most typical example

a deed hailed as the _____ of valor

18. retrogress
(re trə 'gres)

(*v.*) to move backward; to return to an earlier condition

has _____ into barbarism

19. scrutinize
('skrüt ə nīz)

(*v.*) to examine closely

_____ the documents

20. tepid
('tep id)

(*adj.*) lukewarm; unenthusiastic, marked by an absence of interest

a cup of _____ tea

Completing the Sentence

From the words for this unit, choose the one that best completes each of the following sentences. Write the word in the space provided.

1. As the old soldier watched the parade pass by, he was suddenly filled with

_____ for the youthful years he had spent in the Army.

2. An expert from the museum _____ the painting, looking for telltale signs that would prove it to be genuine or expose it as a forgery.

3. My teacher counseled me to keep up my studies, or my performance in

class might once again _____ into mediocrity.

4. Only when we learned that the embezzler had tried to cast suspicion on

his innocent partner did we realize the extent of his _____ .

5. The physical education instructor _____ the virtues of regular exercise.

6. If you are _____ to hard study and intensive reading, how do you expect to get through law school?

7. King Arthur's Knights of the Round Table were the _____ of chivalry.

8. We must not forget the millions of people who were ruthlessly slaughtered

by the Nazis in the _____ of the 1940s.

9. Miss De Carlo's records—neat, accurate, and complete in every respect—

show that she is a most _____ worker.

10. For centuries, Switzerland has avoided becoming a(n) _____ in the wars that have scarred the rest of Europe.

11. Looking forward to a hot bath, I was disappointed at the feeble stream of _____ water that flowed into the tub.

12. Percy shows no particular talent as a worker, but I must admit that he is exceptionally _____ at finding excuses for not doing his job.

13. My teammates agreed that a triple reverse looked mighty impressive on the chalkboard but doubted that the play would prove _____ on the football field.

14. If, as you claim, you really like raw oysters, why do you make such an eloquent _____ every time you swallow one?

15. When I realized how bad the brakes of the old car were, I feared that our lives were in _____ .

16. No one doubts the _____ intentions of the program for community improvement, but it was ruined by mismanagement.

17. When I heard Rose speaking French so fluently, my determination to master that language received a fresh _____ .

18. Regarding native Americans as "bloodthirsty savages," Europeans were rarely able to maintain _____ relations with them.

19. A(n) _____ examination of my luggage was enough to show me that someone had been tampering with it.

20. What good is a plastic raincoat that is _____ to water if it also prevents any body heat from escaping?

Synonyms   *From the words for this unit, choose the one that is most nearly **the same** in meaning as each of the following groups of expressions. Write the word on the line given.*

1. quick, superficial, perfunctory   _____

2. careful, fastidious, painstaking, fussy   _____

3. risk, hazard, peril   _____

4. workable, practicable, viable   _____

5. to revert; to degenerate, decline   _____

6. fraud, double-dealing, chicanery   _____

7. a conflagration; devastation; annihilation _____

8. a longing for things past; homesickness

9. impenetrable; resistant, proof against

10. an impulse, incentive, stimulus, spur

11. disinclined, opposed, loath

12. congenial, neighborly, cordial

13. a pained expression, facial contortion

14. lukewarm; insipid; halfhearted, wishy-washy

15. the purest essence; a paragon, exemplar

16. kindly, benign, well-meaning

17. to inspect, examine, pore over

18. clever, deft, dexterous, slick

19. to glorify, applaud, acclaim, hail

20. assertive, truculent, pugnacious

Antonyms   *From the words for this unit, choose the one that is most nearly **opposite** in meaning to each of the following groups of expressions. Write the word on the line given.*

1. to criticize, belittle, disparage

2. safety, security

3. unworkable, impractical

4. thorough, painstaking, careful

5. a curb, hindrance, impediment, constraint

6. favorably disposed, eager, keen

7. heated, excited, enthusiastic

8. hostile, antagonistic

9. to skim, scan, glance at

10. clumsy, inept, all thumbs

11. malicious, spiteful, malevolent

12. to advance, evolve, progress

13. peaceful, conciliatory, placid

14. porous, permeable, vulnerable

15. careless, negligent, sloppy

16. a deluge, inundation

17. to smile, beam, grin

Choosing the Right Word   *Encircle the **boldface** word that more satisfactorily completes each of the following sentences.*

1. Because I was not even born when the Beatles were at the height of their popularity, their albums do not fill me with (**duplicity, nostalgia**).

2. Though it may appear rather ordinary to the casual observer, Lincoln's Gettysburg Address is to me the (**impetus, quintessence**) of eloquence.

3. Some civil engineers believe that within a generation it will be (**feasible, benevolent**) to derive a large part of our energy directly from the sun.

4. The nightmare that continues to haunt all thoughtful people is a nuclear (**holocaust, jeopardy**) in which our civilization might be destroyed.

5. It made me very uncomfortable to see with what suspicion the wary customs officer (**scrutinized, extolled**) my passport.

6. In the Sherlock Holmes stories, we read of the evil Professor Moriarty, whose (**duplicity, impetus**) was almost a match for Holmes's genius.

7. Though peace talks began with an exchange of lofty sentiments, they soon (**retrogressed, scrutinized**) into petty squabbling and backbiting.

8. I knew she would be (**impervious, meticulous**) in caring for my plants, but I didn't expect her to water them with a medicine dropper!

9. Anyone who is (**averse, cursory**) to having a girls' basketball team in our school doesn't know what's been happening in recent years.

10. (**Extolling, Scrutinizing**) other people's achievements is fine, but it is no substitute for doing something remarkable of your own.

11. Providing a powerful defense force for our nation does not mean that we are taking a (**belligerent, meticulous**) attitude toward any other nation.

12. When I saw my sister land in a tree on her first parachute jump, my interest in learning to skydive became decidedly (**tepid, adroit**).

13. After shouting at each other rather angrily, the participants in the round-table discussion calmed down and parted (**feasibly, amicably**).

14. It was rude of you to (**retrogress, grimace**) so obviously when the speaker mispronounced words and made grammatical errors.

15. The lawyer's (**adroit, cursory**) questioning slowly but surely revealed the weaknesses in his opponent's case.

16. Carelessness in even minor details may (**averse, jeopardize**) the success of a major theatrical production.

17. News of famine in various parts of the world has given added (**nostalgia, impetus**) to the drive to increase food production.

18. His parents tried to encourage an interest in literature, music, and art, but he seemed (**amicable, impervious**) to such influences.

19. Do you think you are being fair in passing judgment on Fran's poem after such a (**cursory, benevolent**) reading?

20. On the morning of the picnic, the sky was gray and overcast, but suddenly the sun came out and smiled on us (**benevolently, adroitly**).

Unit 3

Definitions

Note carefully the spelling, pronunciation, and definition of each of the following words. Then write the word in the blank space in the illustrative phrase following.

1. **adversary**
   ('ad vər ser ē)

   (*n.*) an enemy, opponent

   a worthy _____ on the court

2. **alienate**
   ('ā lē ə nāt)

   (*v.*) to turn away; to make indifferent or hostile; to transfer, convey

   bad habits that _____ friends

3. **artifice**
   ('är tə fis)

   (*n.*) a skillful or ingenious device; a clever trick; clever skill; trickery

   deceived by his _____

4. **coerce**
   (kō 'ərs)

   (*v.*) to compel, force

   _____ into obedience by a threat of punishment

5. **craven**
   ('krā vən)

   (*adj.*) cowardly; (*n.*) a coward

   criticized by his opponent for his _____ policies

6. **culinary**
   ('kyü lə ner ē)

   (*adj.*) of or related to cooking or to the kitchen

   a fine example of French _____ art

7. **delete**
   (di 'lēt)

   (*v.*) to erase, wipe out, cut out

   shortened the report by _____ two paragraphs

8. **demise**
   (di 'mīz)

   (*n.*) a death, especially of a person in a lofty position

   tolling bells that indicated the _____ of the king

9. **exhilarate**
   (eg 'zil ə rāt)

   (*v.*) to enliven, cheer, give spirit or liveliness to

   _____ by the good news

10. **fallow**
    ('fal ō)

    (*adj.*) plowed but not seeded; inactive; reddish-yellow; (*n.*) land left unseeded; (*v.*) to plow but not seed

    garden plots left _____ for a year

11. **harass**
    (hə 'ras)

    (*v.*) to disturb, worry; to trouble by repeated attacks

    _____ the witness with difficult questions

12. **inclement**
    (in 'klem ənt)

    (*adj.*) stormy, harsh; severe in attitude or action

    unaccustomed to the _____ New England winter

13. **muse**
    (myüz)

    (*v.*) to think about in a dreamy way, ponder

    _____ on the meaning of life

14. **negligible**
('neg lə jə bəl)

(*adj.*) so unimportant that it can be disregarded

a _____ loss that we need not worry about

15. **perpetuate**
(pər 'pech ü āt)

(*v.*) to make permanent or long lasting

_____ the customs of our ancestors

16. **precedent**
('pres ə dənt)

(*n.*) an example that may serve as a basis for imitation or later action

set a _____ for others to follow

17. **punitive**
('pyü nə tiv)

(*adj.*) inflicting or aiming at punishment

led a _____ expedition against the rebels

18. **redress**
(rē 'dres)

(*v.*) to set right, remedy; (*n.*) relief from wrong or injury

seek _____ through the courts

19. **sojourn**
('sō jərn)

(*n.*) a temporary stay; (*v.*) to stay for a time

a week's _____ in Paris

20. **urbane**
(ər 'bān)

(*adj.*) refined in manner or style, suave

an _____ host

Completing the Sentence

From the words for this unit, choose the one that best completes each of the following sentences. Write the word in the space provided.

1. Coach Groh took me off the starting team as a(n) _____ measure for missing two days of practice.

2. The deserted buildings and the fields lying _____ hinted at the troubles the farmers in the area were undergoing.

3. When the snowstorm lasted into a second day, we listened attentively to the radio to find out if our school was among those closed because of the

   _____ weather.

4. David's charmingly _____ manner and keen wit made him a much sought-after guest at social gatherings.

5. The _____ of an administration in the United States is never a crisis because a newly elected administration is waiting to take over.

6. The full extent of my _____ skill is preparing scrambled eggs on toast.

7. When planning our trip to the Southwest, we made sure to set aside two

   days for a(n) _____ at the Grand Canyon.

8. Since both cars had virtually come to a halt by the time their bumpers met,

   the damage was _____ .

9. Their _____ behavior at the first sign of danger was a disgrace to the uniform they wore.

10. When citizens feel that something is wrong, they have a right under the First Amendment to ask their government for a(n) _____ of grievances.

11. I advise you to _____ from your statement all the words that people are likely to find personally offensive.

12. In 1858, Abraham Lincoln held a series of debates with Stephen Douglas, his _____ in the contest for U.S. Senator from Illinois.

13. The coach emphasized that the way to stop our opponent's passing game was to _____ their receivers and "blitz" their quarterback.

14. When Grandfather stubbornly refused to eat his vegetables, he set a(n) _____ that was immediately followed by the children.

15. His bad manners and insufferable conceit _____ even those who were most inclined to judge him favorably.

16. If we continue to elect unworthy people to public office, we will simply _____ the evils that we have tried so hard to correct.

17. Magicians rely on sleight of hand and other forms of _____ to deceive their unsuspecting audiences.

18. There are far more subtle ways of _____ a person into doing what you want than twisting his or her arm.

19. As he lay under the old apple tree, he began to _____ on the strange twists of fate that had led to the present situation.

20. At first we watched the game with relatively little emotion, but we became so _____ by our team's strong comeback that we began to cheer loudly.

Synonyms From the words for this unit, choose the one that is most nearly **the same** in meaning as each of the following groups of expressions. Write the word on the line provided at the right.

1. to stimulate, excite, gladden _____

2. blustery, tempestuous, implacable _____

3. fearful, fainthearted, pusillanimous _____

4. suave, elegant _____

5. an antagonist, rival, foe _____

6. to annoy, pester, bedevil, beleaguer, worry _____

7. to rectify, correct, mitigate   _____

8. trivial, inconsequential, insignificant   _____

9. to remove, cancel, expunge   _____

10. penalizing, retaliatory   _____

11. to meditate, contemplate, daydream   _____

12. to separate, drive apart, estrange   _____

13. a visit, stopover, brief stay   _____

14. unproductive, inert, dormant   _____

15. to continue, preserve, prolong indefinitely   _____

16. a death, decease, passing away   _____

17. to pressure, bully, intimidate, constrain   _____

18. a guide, tradition, model   _____

19. a ruse, stratagem, contrivance   _____

20. related to cooking   _____

Antonyms   _From the words for this unit, choose the one that is most nearly_ **opposite** _in meaning to each of the following groups of expressions. Write the word on the line provided at the right._

1. crude, uncouth, boorish   _____

2. brave, courageous, valiant   _____

3. significant, crucial, momentous   _____

4. discourage, dispirit, dishearten, inhibit   _____

5. mild, gentle, balmy, tranquil   _____

6. a friend, ally, supporter, confederate   _____

7. to discontinue, abolish, abandon   _____

8. to befriend, attract, captivate; to reconcile   _____

9. productive, fertile, prolific   _____

10. to insert, add, retain, include   _____

11. a birth, beginning, commencement   _____

12. that which follows or comes afterward   _____

13. to persuade, cajole   _____

Choosing the Right Word   *Encircle the **boldface** word that more satisfactorily completes each of the following sentences.*

1. After a long (**urbane, fallow**) period during which she scarcely touched her brushes, the painter suddenly produced a series of major canvases.

2. May I remind you that the (**punitive, urbane**) action we are authorized to take does not include physical force of any kind.

3. We must reject the (**craven, fallow**) advice of those who feel we can solve social problems by abandoning our democratic freedoms.

4. It is all very well to (**muse, perpetuate**) on what might have happened, but far better to take action to make good things happen.

5. The critics unanimously praised the actor for the (**urbane, negligible**) charm with which he played the well-bred English gentleman.

6. When Washington refused to serve a third term as President, he set a(n) (**precedent, artifice**) that was to last for 150 years.

7. We need a foreman who can maintain good discipline in the shop without (**harassing, exhilarating**) the workers.

8. Because of the severe sentences he often handed down, he gained the reputation of being an extremely (**inclement, negligible**) judge.

9. I want to know by whose authority my name was (**deleted, coerced**) from the list of students eligible to take the scholarship examinations.

10. When he blocked my jump shot, took the rebound, drove down the court, and scored, I realized that I was facing a worthy (**artifice, adversary**).

11. If we do not take steps now to clear his name, we will be (**perpetuating, redressing**) an injustice that has already lasted far too long.

12. Our city government needs basic reforms; clever little (**precedents, artifices**) will not solve our problems.

13. I admit that we did some foolish things after the game, but you must remember how (**mused, exhilarated**) we were by the victory.

14. Do you really expect me to believe that your friends (**coerced, alienated**) you into cutting class to go to the movies?

15. Only when the attempt to get the British government to (**redress, harass**) injustices proved unsuccessful did the American colonists resort to arms.

16. Our history shows how the (**demise, artifice**) of one political party provides an opportunity for the formation of a new one.

17. The highlight of my trip to Europe came when I (**sojourned, redressed**) in the birthplace of my ancestors.

18. And now I want you all to try my (**inclement, culinary**) masterpiece—a salami souffle, garnished with sour cream.

19. Since we are making (**negligible, craven**) progress in our fight against pollution, the time has come for us to adopt completely new methods.

20. Coach Gates ran the risk of (**exhilarating, alienating**) influential graduates of the school when he suspended a star player who had broken training.

Analogies *In each of the following, encircle the item that best completes the comparison.*

1. **dour** is to **cheery** as
a. stolid is to impervious
b. amicable is to pliable
c. fallow is to productive
d. inclement is to belligerent

2. **averse** is to **reluctant** as
a. adroit is to dexterous
b. insidious is to benevolent
c. verbatim is to oral
d. culinary is to tepid

3. **delete** is to **insert** as
a. muse is to ponder
b. decrease is to augment
c. harass is to frighten
d. coerce is to compel

4. **duplicity** is to **unfavorable** as
a. fortitude is to favorable
b. intimation is to unfavorable
c. demise is to favorable
d. precedent is to unfavorable

5. **adversary** is to **friendly** as
a. peacemaker is to belligerent
b. juggler is to ambidextrous
c. orphan is to bereft
d. coward is to craven

6. **meticulous** is to **cursory** as
a. adulterated is to unkempt
b. warily is to cautiously
c. appreciable is to negligible
d. tentative is to feasible

7. **unkempt** is to **appearance** as
a. tepid is to height
b. urbane is to manner
c. impervious is to complexion
d. stolid is to weight

8. **virtue** is to **extol** as
a. accomplishment is to gibe
b. duplicity is to honor
c. right is to redress
d. vice is to deplore

9. **lawyer** is to **legal** as
a. sculptor is to naval
b. politician is to punitive
c. athlete is to intellectual
d. chef is to culinary

10. **gape** is to **wide** as
a. yawn is to narrow
b. frown is to wide
c. squint is to narrow
d. blink is to wide

11. **nostalgia** is to **sad** as
a. adversity is to joyful
b. impetus is to sad
c. exhilaration is to joyful
d. guise is to sad

12. **insidious** is to **unfavorable** as
a. benevolent is to favorable
b. meticulous is to unfavorable
c. craven is to favorable
d. ambidextrous is to unfavorable

13. **hovel** is to **poverty** as
a. apartment is to artifice
b. palace is to opulence
c. fort is to jeopardy
d. cave is to quintessence

14. **flood** is to **water** as
a. avalanche is to wind
b. holocaust is to fire
c. hurricane is to ice
d. tornado is to snow

15. **precedent** is to **before** as
a. intimation is to after
b. redress is to before
c. consequence is to after
d. retrogression is to before

16. **smile** is to **grimace** as
a. laugh is to cry
b. sneeze is to yawn
c. weep is to bewail
d. wink is to blink

17. **reiterate** is to **repeat** as
a. extol is to criticize
b. perpetuate is to commit
c. scrutinize is to muse
d. deploy is to arrange

18. **sponge** is to **impervious** as
a. glass is to brittle
b. wall is to rigid
c. umbrella is to porous
d. belt is to pliable

Identification   *In each of the following groups, encircle the word that is best defined or suggested by the introductory phrase.*

1. stare at in amazement
a. gape   b. grimace   c. redress   d. harass

2. emphasize by repetition
a. scrutinize   b. reiterate   c. gibe   d. tepid

3. not easily moved to emotion
a. meticulous   b. stolid   c. impervious   d. feasible

4. a deceptive appearance
a. nostalgia   b. redress   c. craven   d. guise

5. showing extreme attention to details
a. meticulous   b. adroit   c. punitive   d. negligible

6. one step forward, two steps back
a. reiterate   b. ambidextrous   c. retrogress   d. delete

7. "The King is dead. Long live the King!"
a. jeopardy   b. demise   c. duplicity   d. adversary

8. a facial expression that shows a negative reaction
a. redress   b. grimace   c. artifice   d. intimation

9. "That guy is chickenhearted."
a. fortitude   b. adversary   c. verbatim   d. craven

10. how one might characterize the prosecution and the defense in a legal suit
a. muses   b. intimations   c. precedents   d. adversaries

11. harmful, but in a rather attractive way
a. insidious   b. cursory   c. heedless   d. dour

12. the purest of the pure
a. nostalgia   b. artifice   c. intimation   d. quintessence

13. said of a "double-dealer"
a. intimation   b. duplicity   c. precedent   d. adversary

14. look over carefully and critically
a. perpetuate   b. scrutinize   c. alienate   d. reiterate

15. payment for a scratched fender from the person responsible
a. redress   b. fortitude   c. holocaust   d. grimace

16. tease with mocking words
a. muse   b. delete   c. coerce   d. gibe

17. neither hot nor cold
a. craven   b. averse   c. tepid   d. ambidextrous

18. a one-week stay in Athens
a. sojourn   b. precedent   c. reiteration   d. jeopardy

19. cause to last indefinitely
a. provoke   b. harass   c. coerce   d. perpetuate

20. driving force
a. jeopardy   b. nostalgia   c. grimace   d. impetus

Shades of Meaning   *Read each sentence carefully. Then encircle the item that best completes the statement below the sentence.*

Only a complete megalomaniac would maintain such an opulent view of his own importance to the order of things.   (2)

1. In line 1 the word **opulent** is used to mean
   a. wealthy
   b. grandiose
   c. progressive
   d. abundant

"The Raven" and "The Tell-Tale Heart" prove that Poe, in T.S. Eliot's memorable phrase, was "ambidextrous in prose and verse."   (2)

2. The word **ambidextrous** in line 2 most nearly means
   a. twice-told
   b. equally skilled
   c. able to use both hands
   d. doubly literate

In some ancient societies prisoners of war figured prominently in the elaborate holocausts that marked major religious festivals.   (2)

3. The word **holocausts** in line 2 is best defined as
   a. human sacrifices
   b. religious ceremonies
   c. theological disputes
   d. burnt offerings

In their steep mountain fastnesses clan leaders were impervious to attack, even from "technologically advanced" enemies like Rome.   (2)

4. In line 1 the phrase **impervious to** most nearly means
   a. safe from
   b. prepared for
   c. unmoved by
   d. subject to

After years of fallow in his life, a series of brilliant military triumphs catapulted the general into national prominence.   (2)

5. The word **fallow** in line 1 can best be defined as
   a. unused land
   b. preparation
   c. inactivity
   d. a reddish-yellow color

Antonyms   *In each of the following groups, encircle the word or expression that is most nearly the **opposite** of the first word in **boldface type**.*

1. adulterate
a. lose
b. harass
c. purify
d. cheat

2. extol
a. improve
b. criticize
c. charge
d. analyze

3. cursory
a. blasphemous
b. brave
c. speedy
d. thorough

4. craven
a. stuffed
b. yielding
c. brave
d. tidy

5. adroit
a. friendly
b. bereft
c. smooth
d. clumsy

6. feasible
a. cheap
b. glum
c. impractical
d. delicious

7. inclement
a. pleasant
b. strange
c. boring
d. tasty

8. warily
a. rashly
b. softly
c. quietly
d. angrily

9. amicable	**12. verbatim**	**15. augment**	**18. pliable**
a. quarrelsome	a. nominal	a. insult	a. consumable
b. friendly	b. pleasing	b. reduce	b. straight
c. easy	c. adapted	c. predict	c. demanding
d. intellectual	d. delayed	d. annoy	d. rigid
10. adversary	**13. urbane**	**16. unkempt**	**19. retrogress**
a. accuser	a. crude	a. bound	a. agree
b. enemy	b. rural	b. punctual	b. advance
c. relative	c. weak	c. neat	c. eject
d. ally	d. irrelevant	d. shiny	d. permit
11. perpetuate	**14. opulent**	**17. exhilarate**	**20. averse**
a. soothe	a. unkind	a. accuse	a. favorable
b. discontinue	b. wretched	b. depress	b. safe
c. anger	c. rich	c. excite	c. unwilling
d. commit	d. small	d. worsen	d. joyous

Completing the Sentence

From the following list of words choose the one that best completes each of the sentences below. Write the word in the appropriate space.

Group A

bereft	**impetus**	**precedent**	**inclement**
guise	**jeopardy**	**holocaust**	**ambidextrous**
stolid	**intimation**	**grimace**	**averse**

1. There is no historical _____ for the new policy she proposes to introduce.

2. The children's efforts to _____ like little devils produced more amusement than terror in bystanders.

3. Raincoats and rubbers seem the only sensible apparel in such _____ weather.

4. The speaker warned that unless we can find adequate and dependable sources of energy, the very existence of our society may be placed in _____ .

5. When he told me of his recent conversation with Yvonne, I had my first _____ of why I had not been invited to the party.

Group B

impervious	**belligerent**	**artifice**	**extol**
scrutinize	**alienated**	**insidious**	**tepid**
duplicity	**nostalgia**	**gape**	**gibes**

1. After finishing the last problem, I carefully _____ the entire exam for any errors I might have overlooked.

2. Her tone was so _____ that I was afraid she planned to give me a poke in the eye.

3. Thanks to the recent earthquake, "There _____ a mighty crater/Where solid rock once stood." (A.E. Glug, "Rumblings," 1)

4. She bore their _____ with such good nature and patience that they soon gave up and looked for someone else to make fun of.

5. We must be prepared to resist the _____ influence of his disguised racial prejudice.

Word Families

A. *On the line provided write a* **noun form** *of each of the following words.*

EXAMPLE: insidious—**insidiousness**

1. retrogress _____

2. feasible _____

3. perpetuate _____

4. adroit _____

5. tentative _____

6. warily _____

7. opulent _____

8. harass _____

9. benevolent _____

10. adulterate _____

11. urbane _____

12. scrutinize _____

13. alienate _____

14. coerce _____

15. delete _____

16. exhilarate _____

B. *On the line provided, write a* **verb** *related to each of the following words.*

EXAMPLE: precedent—**precede**

1. intimation _____

2. negligible _____

3. bereft _____

4. jeopardy _____

5. punitive _____

**Filling
the Blanks**

*Encircle the pair of words that best complete the
meaning of each of the following passages.*

1. "I haven't yet had the time to give your latest sales report more than a
_____ glance," my boss told me. "However, I plan to
_____ it carefully before we sit down to discuss it in detail."
   a. verbatim . . . reiterate
   b. cursory . . . scrutinize
   c. meticulous . . . augment
   d. tentative . . . redress

2. Tony's general attitude toward people is so _____ that he
has _____ absolutely everybody who knows him. If he didn't
walk around with such a huge chip on his shoulder, he would have a few
friends.
   a. benevolent . . . deployed
   b. adversary . . . exhilarated
   c. belligerent . . . alienated
   d. amicable . . . redressed

3. Some people always stick up their noses at food they're not accustomed
to, but I'm not at all _____ to trying something new. Still,
experience has taught me to be _____ of such dubious
delicacies as chocolate-covered ants, and I usually "look before I leap,"
so to speak.
   a. amicable . . . bereft
   b. tepid . . . negligible
   c. averse . . . wary
   d. impervious . . . craven

4. I want to use an excerpt from the President's inaugural address in my
report. Unfortunately, the passage I want is far too long to reproduce
_____ . To get it down to the size I need, I'll have to
_____ part of it.
   a. tentatively . . . augment
   b. stolidly . . . coerce
   c. meticulously . . . reiterate
   d. verbatim . . . delete

5. My first _____ of Nelson's double-dealing came when I
discovered him whispering with my opponent. Prior to that, I had no inkling
of my so-called friend's _____ .
   a. intimation . . . duplicity
   b. scrutiny . . . fortitude
   c. precedent . . . artifice
   d. redress . . . coercion

6. Because the course of the disease was so _____ , we
didn't notice at first that the patient's condition was no longer improving
but in fact had begun to _____ .
   a. tentative . . . adulterate
   b. adroit . . . redress
   c. averse . . . perpetuate
   d. insidious . . . retrogress

Unit 4

Definitions *Note carefully the spelling, pronunciation, and definition of each of the following words. Then write the word in the blank space in the illustrative phrase following.*

1. affiliated
(ə 'fil ē āt əd)
(*adj., part.*) associated, connected
_____ with a well-known law firm

2. ascertain
(as ər 'tān)
(*v.*) to find out
_____ what the cost will be

3. attainment
(ə 'tān mənt)
(*n.*) an accomplishment; the act of achieving
a man of high literary _____

4. bequeath
(bi 'kwēth)
(*v.*) to give or pass on as an inheritance
has _____ a fortune to his widow

5. cogent
('kō jint)
(*adj.*) forceful, convincing; relevant, to the point
a _____ plea for prison reform

6. converge
(kən 'verj)
(*v.*) to move toward one point, approach nearer together
as the delegates _____ on the hall

7. disperse
(di 'spərs)
(*v.*) to scatter, spread far and wide
order the police to _____ the crowd

8. esteem
(es 'tēm)
(*v.*) to regard highly; (*n.*) a highly favorable opinion or judgment
someone we all hold in high _____

9. expunge
(ik 'spənj)
(*v.*) to erase, obliterate, destroy
ordered the offending remarks _____ from the court record

10. finite
('fī nīt)
(*adj.*) having limits; lasting for a limited time
a _____ number of possibilities

11. invulnerable
(in 'vəl nər ə bəl)
(*adj.*) not able to be wounded or hurt; shielded against attack
an _____ fortress

12. malevolent
(mə 'lev ə lənt)
(*adj.*) spiteful, showing ill will
told a _____ lie

13. nonchalant
(nän shə 'länt)
(*adj.*) cool and confident, unconcerned
walked down the street with a _____ air

14. omniscient
(äm 'nish ənt)
(*adj.*) knowing everything; having unlimited awareness or understanding
a professor who seemed to be _____

15. panacea
(pan ə 'sē ə)

(*n.*) a remedy for all ills, cure-all; an answer to all problems

a _____ for all our problems

16. scrupulous
('skrü pyə ləs)

(*adj.*) exact, careful, attending thoroughly to details; having high moral standards, principled

describe with _____ accuracy

17. skulk
(skəlk)

(*v.*) to move about stealthily; to lie in hiding

a burglar _____ in an alley

18. supercilious
(sü pər 'sil ē əs)

(*adj.*) proud and contemptuous; showing scorn because of a feeling of superiority

took a _____ attitude toward the servants

19. uncanny
(ən 'kan ē)

(*adj.*) strange, mysterious, weird, beyond explanation

an _____ skill at playing bridge

20. venial
('vē nē əl)

(*adj.*) easily excused; pardonable

a _____ offense

Completing the Sentence

From the words for this unit, choose the one that best completes each of the following sentences. Write the word in the space provided.

1. Her ability to guess what I am thinking about at any given time is nothing short of _____ .

2. So long as we remained indoors, we were _____ to the Arctic blasts that swept down on our snowbound cabin.

3. The more knowledge and wisdom people acquire, the more keenly they become aware that no one is _____ .

4. Because our natural resources are _____ and by no means inexhaustible, we must learn to conserve them.

5. We refer to antibiotics as "wonder drugs," but we must realize that they are not _____ for all the physical ailments of mankind.

6. Our representative offered one simple but _____ argument against the proposal—it would raise the cost of living.

7. Isn't it remarkable how quickly a throng of sunbathers will pick up their belongings and _____ when a few drops of rain fall?

8. Is there anyone in the world as _____ as a senior who attends a mere sophomore class dance?

9. Her election to Congress was the _____ of a lifelong ambition.

10. As we stood on the railway tracks looking off into the distance, the rails seemed to _____ and meet at some far-off point.

11. Only by paying _____ attention to innumerable details were we able to piece together the cause of the accident.

12. The screening committee investigated not only the candidate himself but also the organizations with which he was _____ .

13. Before making our final plans, we should _____ exactly how much money we will have for expenses.

14. Though I wanted to "let bygones be bygones," I found that I could not wholly _____ the bitter memory of their behavior from my mind.

15. When I saw the pain he caused others and the pleasure he took in doing so, I realized he was a truly _____ person.

16. If only parents could _____ their hard-won practical wisdom and experience to their children!

17. In a situation that would have left me all but helpless with embarrassment, he remained cool and _____ .

18. I knew the dean would accept my apology when she characterized my behavior as thoughtless but _____ .

19. When the candidate admitted openly that he had been mistaken in some of his earlier policies, we _____ him more highly than ever.

20. In the opening scene of the horror film a shadowy figure dressed in black _____ through the graveyard in the moonlight.

Synonyms   *From the words for this unit, choose the one that is most nearly **the same** in meaning as each of the following groups of expressions. Write the word on the line provided at the right.*

1. snobbish, patronizing, overbearing   _____

2. painstaking, meticulous, conscientious   _____

3. composed, unruffled, indifferent, blasé   _____

4. to lurk, slink, prowl   _____

5. to hand down, transmit, bestow   _____

6. to respect, admire, honor, revere   _____

7. malicious, wicked, sinister, malignant   _____

8. impregnable, impervious, immune _____

9. eerie, inexplicable, spooky _____

10. attached, related, joined to _____

11. to meet, unite, intersect, merge _____

12. a universal cure; an easy solution _____

13. to delete, efface, annihilate _____

14. persuasive, compelling _____

15. wise, all-knowing _____

16. excusable, forgivable _____

17. to discover, determine, establish, find out _____

18. limited, bounded, measurable _____

19. an achievement, fulfillment _____

20. to break up, scatter, dispel _____

Antonyms *From the words for this unit, choose the one that is most nearly **opposite** in meaning to each of the following groups of expressions. Write the word on the line provided at the right.*

1. ignorant, unknowing _____

2. careless, negligent, remiss; dishonest _____

3. disdain, scorn, contempt _____

4. kind, benevolent, compassionate _____

5. a failure, defeat; frustration _____

6. to collect, congregate, assemble, muster _____

7. exposed, unprotected, defenseless _____

8. unlimited, immeasurable; everlasting, eternal _____

9. humble, meek, deferential, servile _____

10. perturbed, agitated, disconcerted, abashed _____

11. unconvincing, weak, ineffective; irrelevant _____

12. unpardonable, unforgivable, inexcusable _____

13. unconnected, dissociated _____

14. to diverge, separate, go separate ways _____

15. to insert; to mark, imprint, impress _____

Choosing the Right Word   *Encircle the **boldface** word that more satisfactorily completes each of the following sentences.*

1. At first, the two candidates were in disagreement on every issue, but as the campaign went on, their opinions seemed to (**disperse, converge**).

2. Is it true that some dogs have a(n) (**uncanny, malevolent**) sense of the approach of death?

3. When I found myself flushed with anger, I realized that I was not so (**scrupulous, invulnerable**) to his bitter sarcasm as I had thought I was!

4. Though Mr. Darden has spent years studying African history, he does not claim to be (**omniscient, cogent**) in that field.

5. The critic recognized the book's faults but dismissed them as (**venial, uncanny**) in view of the author's overall achievement.

6. As a member of the grand jury, it is your duty to be (**supercilious, scrupulous**) in weighing every detail of evidence.

7. The reform candidate vowed to root out the corruption that (**bequeathed, skulked**) through the corridors of City Hall.

8. The newspaper revealed that the city's chief building inspector was (**converged, affiliated**) with a large construction company.

9. Her elegant clothes and (**finite, supercilious**) manner did not conceal the fact that she was our old friend, Beulah Blitz, a former waitress.

10. Instead of making an "informed guess," why not (**ascertain, esteem**) exactly how many students are going on the trip to Washington?

11. Lincoln said, "If you once forfeit the confidence of your fellow citizens, you can never regain their respect and (**esteem, attainment**)."

12. We found her criticism of our conduct unpleasant, but we had to admit that her remarks were (**venial, cogent**).

13. Instead of blaming a (**malevolent, invulnerable**) fate for your failures, why not look for the causes within yourself?

14. There are so many different factors involved in an energy crisis that no single measure can be expected to serve as a(n) (**panacea, attainment**).

15. He is the kind of person who has many (**convergences, attainments**) but seems unable to put them to any practical use.

16. Nothing he may (**disperse, bequeath**) to the next generation can be more precious than the memory of his long life of honorable public service.

17. Though the journey seemed interminable, I knew that it was (**cogent, finite**) and that I would soon be home.

18. Her bright, optimistic manner did much to (**converge, disperse**) the atmosphere of gloom that had settled over the meeting.

19. When I splattered paint on my art teacher, I tried to appear (**nonchalant, malevolent**) but succeeded only in looking horrified.

20. Scientists still debate whether it was a sudden catastrophe or a natural process that (**expunged, converged**) dinosaurs from the face of the earth.

Unit 5

Definitions

Note carefully the spelling, pronunciation, and definition of each of the following words. Then write the word in the blank space in the illustrative phrase following.

1. altruistic
(al trü 'is tik)

(*adj.*) unselfish, concerned with the welfare of others

an _____ program to help the poor

2. assent
(ə 'sent)

(*v.*) to express agreement; (*n.*) agreement

forced to _____ to their demands

3. benefactor
('ben ə fak tər)

(*n.*) one who does good to others

became my _____ in time of need

4. chivalrous
('shiv əl rəs)

(*adj.*) marked by honor, courtesy, and courage; knightly

praised for this _____ act

5. clemency
('klem ən sē)

(*n.*) mercy, humaneness; mildness, moderateness

show _____ to first offenders

6. dearth
(dərth)

(*n.*) a lack, scarcity, inadequate supply; a famine

a _____ of able assistants

7. diffident
('dif ə dənt)

(*adj.*) shy, lacking self-confidence; modest, reserved

amused by the _____ suitor

8. discrepancy
(dis 'krep ən sē)

(*n.*) a difference; a lack of agreement

a _____ between their stories

9. embark
(em 'bärk)

(*v.*) to go aboard; to make a start; to invest

_____ on the long ocean trip

10. facile
('fas əl)

(*adj.*) easily done or attained; superficial; ready, fluent; easily shown but not sincerely felt

a _____ writer

11. indomitable
(in 'däm ət ə bəl)

(*adj.*) unconquerable, refusing to yield

admire her _____ courage

12. infallible
(in 'fal ə bəl)

(*adj.*) free from error; absolutely dependable

his _____ judgment

13. plod
(pläd)

(*v.*) to walk heavily or slowly; to work slowly

_____ wearily through the snow

14. pungent
('pən jənt)

(*adj.*) causing a sharp sensation; stinging, biting

the _____ odor of onion soup

15. remiss
(rē 'mis)

(*adj.*) neglectful in performance of one's duty, careless

_____ in doing daily chores

16. repose
(rē 'pōz)

(*v.*) to rest; lie; place; (*n.*) relaxation; peace of mind, calmness

a much-needed period of _____

17. temerity
(tə 'mer ə tē)
(*n.*) rashness, boldness

have the _____ to answer back

18. truculent
('trək yə lənt)
(*adj.*) fierce and cruel; aggressive; deadly, destructive; scathingly harsh

shocked by his _____ disposition

19. unfeigned
(ən 'fānd)
(*adj.*) sincere, real, without pretense

the _____ emotions of a child

20. virulent
('vir yə lənt)
(*adj.*) extremely poisonous; full of malice, spiteful

a _____ racist

Completing the Sentence

From the words for this unit, choose the one that best completes each of the following sentences. Write the word in the space provided.

1. He is not merely unpleasant but actually dangerous whenever he gets into one of his _____ moods.

2. The pathetic refugees _____ along the dusty road, hoping to reach the Red Cross camp before nightfall.

3. In view of the many able people in public life today, I do not agree that we are suffering from a(n) _____ of capable leaders.

4. His _____ joy when it was announced that I had won the scholarship meant more to me than all the polite congratulations I received.

5. History tells us that many men and women considered "failures" in their own lifetimes were really major _____ of humanity.

6. Humor should be clever and amusing but never so _____ that it hurts the feelings of other people.

7. What good are _____ principles if no real attempt is made to help people by putting them into practice?

8. As soon as the last passenger had _____ , the captain ordered the ship to get underway.

9. As a school cafeteria guard, I would be _____ in my duties if I failed to report any serious disorder.

10. Emphasizing the youth of the convicted man, the defense attorney pleaded for _____ .

11. Do you really think it is _____ to give your seat to a pretty girl when an aged and infirm lady is standing nearby?

12. The brash young lieutenant had the _____ to disregard the express orders of his commanding officer.

13. Paula's parents will not _____ to her going to the dance unless she promises faithfully to be home no later than 1:00 A.M.

14. I did not realize how beautiful the child was until she fell asleep and I saw her face in complete _____ .

15. The custom of putting erasers on pencils is one way of recognizing the fact that no one is _____ .

16. Leonard rarely joins in the discussions, not because he lacks information and ideas but rather because he is _____ .

17. Doctors attributed the epidemic to the rampant spread of a particularly _____ strain of influenza virus.

18. Refusing to admit defeat even when things looked completely hopeless, our _____ football team drove 85 yards in the last few minutes to score the winning touchdown.

19. The principal claimed that there were major _____ between what actually happened in the school and the way the incident had been reported on TV.

20. We were all impressed by his _____ use of unusual words and expressions that he had learned only a few hours before.

21. How the _____ smell of burning leaves in autumn arouses memories of happier days!

Synonyms   *From the words for this unit, choose the one that is most nearly **the same** in meaning as each of the following groups of expressions. Write the word on the line provided at the right.*

1. negligent, lax, slack   _____

2. leniency, forbearance, gentleness   _____

3. timid, bashful; unassertive, withdrawn   _____

4. venomous; noxious, baneful; hateful   _____

5. brutal, savage, belligerent, vitriolic   _____

6. genuine, heartfelt   _____

7. unbeatable, invincible, unyielding   _____

8. gallant, civil; valiant   _____

9. recklessness, foolhardiness; effrontery _____

10. a disagreement, divergence, inconsistency _____

11. to commence, launch, begin; to board   _____

12. sharp, spicy, piquant; caustic; racy   _____

5

13. easy, effortless; assured, poised; specious   _____

14. unerring, certain   _____

15. to concur, agree, consent, accede   _____

16. selfless, rising above personal interests   _____

17. an insufficiency, want, paucity   _____

18. to lumber, trudge   _____

19. sleep; tranquility; a respite   _____

20. one who helps others; a patron, humanitarian   _____

Antonyms   *From the words for this unit, choose the one that is most nearly **opposite** in meaning to each of the following groups of expressions. Write the word on the line provided at the right.*

1. convergence; agreement, consistency   _____

2. scrupulous, dutiful, punctilious   _____

3. open to error, imperfect   _____

4. a surplus, oversupply, glut, abundance   _____

5. to scamper, skip, prance   _____

6. a misanthrope; a malefactor   _____

7. gentle, mild; meek, unthreatening   _____

8. bold, brash, audacious; self-confident, jaunty   _____

9. exertion; wakefulness; tumult, bustle, ado   _____

10. to disagree, differ, dissent   _____

11. innocuous, harmless; benign   _____

12. crude, uncouth, churlish, loutish   _____

13. selfish, self-centered   _____

14. insincere, simulated, phony   _____

15. yielding, surrendering, submissive   _____

16. harshness, severity, cruelty, inflexibility   _____

17. timidity, fearfulness, diffidence, humility   _____

18. labored, awkward, halting   _____

19. bland, unappetizing, colorless, insipid   _____

Choosing the Right Word   *Encircle the **boldface** word that more satisfactorily completes each of the following sentences.*

1. After boasting to me of his family's great wealth, he had the (**clemency, temerity**) to ask me for a loan.

2. By 1781, George Washington's green recruits of a few years earlier had been forged into an (**infallible, indomitable**) army.

3. Lucille is a popular young woman because people realize that her interest in them is sympathetic and (**remiss, unfeigned**).

4. Phil is not too well informed on most matters, but when it comes to big-league baseball, he is all but (**indomitable, infallible**).

5. American Presidents often point to one of their school teachers as the (**discrepancy, benefactor**) who helped shape their character and ideas.

6. I admired his (**remiss, facile**) flow of words, but they failed to convince me that he had practical ideas to help solve our problems.

7. We had no inkling of Calvin's deep-seated aversion to modern pop music until we overheard his (**altruistic, virulent**) comments about punk rock.

8. The lawyer (**plodded, embarked**) through hundreds of pages of the trial record hoping to find some basis for an appeal.

9. In the violent world of today's pro football, good sportsmanship and (**pungent, chivalrous**) behavior still have a place.

10. We soon learned that behind his retiring and (**truculent, diffident**) manner, there was a keen mind and a strong will.

11. As a state legislator, you should not give your (**assent, chivalry**) to any measure unless you truly believe in it.

12. With all the deductions, there is a (**clemency, discrepancy**) of forty dollars between my official salary and my weekly paycheck.

13. Her (**pungent, truculent**) comments during the TV panel show were not only amusing but very much to the point.

14. The planet Earth is a sort of spaceship on which more than five billion of us have (**reposed, embarked**) on a lifelong voyage.

15. In a grim old joke, a man found guilty of murdering his parents appeals for (**clemency, assent**) because he is an orphan.

16. We breathed a sigh of relief when we saw the supposedly missing set of keys (**assenting, reposing**) in the desk drawer.

17. How do you account for the (**clemency, dearth**) of old-fashioned "family doctors" willing to make house calls?

18. Great political leaders know how to appeal to people not only through self-interest but also through their sense of (**temerity, altruism**).

19. You will surely win more support for your view by quiet discussion than by (**chivalrous, truculent**) attacks on your opponents.

20. It would be (**indomitable, remiss**) of me, as editor-in-chief of the school newspaper, not to express appreciation of the help of our faculty advisor.

Unit 6

Definitions

Note carefully the spelling, pronunciation, and definition of each of the following words. Then write the word in the blank space in the illustrative phrase following.

1. accede
(ak 'sēd)

(*v.*) to yield to; to assume an office or dignity

_____ to their reasonable request

2. brandish
('bran dish)

(*v.*) to wave or flourish in a menacing fashion

_____ his cane threateningly

3. comprise
(kəm 'prīz)

(*v.*) to include or contain; to be made up of

a book _____ entirely of essays

4. deft
(deft)

(*adj.*) skillful, nimble

sew with _____ fingers

5. destitute
('des tə tüt)

(*adj.*) deprived of the necessities of life; lacking in

aid to _____ families

6. explicit
(ek 'splis it)

(*adj.*) definite, clearly stated

greatly in need of _____ directions

7. extirpate
('ek stər pāt)

(*v.*) to tear up by the roots; to destroy totally

_____ all forms of racism

8. inopportune
(in äp ər 'tün)

(*adj.*) coming at a bad time; not appropriate

arrive at an _____ time for me

9. ironic
(ī 'rän ik)

(*adj.*) suggesting an incongruity between what might be expected and what actually happens; given to irony, sarcastic

an _____ twist of fate

10. musty
('məs tē)

(*adj.*) stale, moldy; out-of-date

a _____ smell in the closet

11. officious
(ə 'fish əs)

(*adj.*) meddling; excessively forward in offering services or assuming authority

annoyed by the _____ usher

12. ominous
('äm ə nəs)

(*adj.*) unfavorable, threatening, of bad omen

an _____ report from the doctor

13. pinnacle
('pin ə kəl)

(*n.*) a high peak or point

reach the _____ of success

14. premeditated
(prē 'med ə tāt id)

(*adj., part.*) considered beforehand, deliberately planned

guilty of a _____ act of violence

15. rampant
('ram pənt)

(*adj.*) growing without check, running wild

_____ rumors

42

16. solace
('säl əs)

(*n.*) comfort, relief; (*v.*) to comfort, console

find _____ in music

17. stately
('stāt lē)

(*adj.*) dignified, majestic

impressed by the _____ procession

18. supple
('səp əl)

(*adj.*) bending easily; bending with agility; readily adaptable; servile

the sapling's _____ branches

19. suppress
(sə 'pres)

(*v.*) to stop by force, put down

use force to _____ a rebellion

20. venal
('vēn əl)

(*adj.*) open to or marked by bribery or corruption

a _____ official

Completing the Sentence

From the words for this unit, choose the one that best completes each of the following sentences. Write the word in the space provided.

1. A great dancer, like a great athlete, must have a sharp sense of timing and a highly trained, responsive, and _____ body.

2. What a(n) _____ time to ask Milt for help, just when he was having trouble with his own car!

3. The sudden drop in temperature and the unnatural stillness in the air were _____ signs of an unfavorable change in the weather.

4. From 1859 to 1871, "Boss" Tweed controlled New York City through a(n) _____ political machine that fed on graft and extortion.

5. Who would have dreamt that the old attic, with all its darkness, dust, and _____ odor, contained such a treasure!

6. We will never _____ to those selfish and unfair demands.

7. During the darkest hours of defeat, their only _____ was the knowledge that they had fought hard to the very end.

8. Unfortunately, the so-called "recreational facilities" _____ nothing more than a Ping-Pong table and a small-screen TV set.

9. Attacking the present administration, the candidate said that crime has been running _____ in the streets of our city.

10. The unruly mob retreated as the line of deputies moved foward slowly, _____ their riot sticks.

11. Isn't it _____ that he finally inherited all that money at a time when it could no longer help to solve his problems!

12. Even when economic conditions improve, there will still be a large number of _____ families in urgent need of our assistance.

13. It is a truly sobering thought to realize that when one has reached the

_____ of a mountain, there is nowhere to go but down.

14. Who can forget the sight of those _____ "tall ships" with their lofty masts and graceful lines as they sailed past the Statue of Liberty on the Fourth of July?

15. I vowed that I would _____ every weed that dared to show itself in our newly seeded lawn.

16. Whether your act was _____ or the result of carelessness, the fact remains that you have caused great pain to someone who has always been very good to you.

17. Try as we might, we could not _____ our laughter at his clumsy attempts to breakdance to waltz music.

18. The referee showed good judgment in giving a(n) _____ warning that if either team protested his decisions, he would be forced to call a technical foul.

19. I love to watch the _____ movements of little Billy Gomez as he dribbles the ball downcourt and passes off to the taller players.

20. Can I ever forget that _____ clerk in the customs office who insisted that I empty every piece of luggage before him!

Synonyms   *From the words for this unit, choose the one that is most nearly **the same** in meaning as each of the following groups of expressions. Write the word on the line provided at the right.*

1. distinct, forthright, unambiguous   _____

2. preplanned, rehearsed, calculated   _____

3. widespread, unrestrained, extravagant   _____

4. meddlesome, prying, impertinent   _____

5. dexterous, adroit, proficient   _____

6. ill-timed, inconvenient, inappropriate   _____

7. to soothe, reassure, console, comfort   _____

8. stale, hackneyed, antiquated   _____

9. to swing, shake, flourish   _____

10. flexible, limber, pliable   _____

11. unpropitious, inauspicious, portentous   _____

12. bribable, corruptible; mercenary   _____

13. an apex, acme, summit, apogee   _____

44

14. to uproot, eradicate, wipe out _____

15. incongruous; poignant; satiric, sardonic, _____
wry, tongue-in-cheek

16. to subdue, crush, stifle, squelch, quash _____

17. to consent, concur, comply _____

18. grand, magnificent, imposing _____

19. wanting, devoid, impoverished _____

20. to compose, constitute, encompass _____

Antonyms *From the words for this unit, choose the one that is most
nearly **opposite** in meaning to each of the following
groups of expressions. Write the word on the line
provided at the right.*

1. fresh, sweet-smelling; up-to-date, brand-new _____

2. to provoke, spur, arouse, incite, instigate _____

3. auspicious, propitious, promising _____

4. a low point, nadir, perigee _____

5. controlled, restrained, held in check _____

6. timely, convenient, felicitous _____

7. honest, scrupulous, incorruptible _____

8. rich, wealthy; luxurious, bountiful; full, replete _____

9. lowly, humble; servile, abject _____

10. to withhold consent, demur, balk at _____

11. unplanned, spontaneous, impromptu _____

12. vague, ambiguous; implied, implicit _____

13. straightforward, unequivocal, artless _____

14. stiff, rigid; unbending, hidebound _____

15. clumsy, awkward, bungling, inept _____

16. to vex, aggravate, upset _____

17. to implant, sow; to foster, nourish _____

18. to exclude _____

19. reserved, diffident, timid; aloof _____

Choosing the　　*Encircle the **boldface** word that more satisfactorily*
Right Word　　　*completes each of the following sentences.*

1. He is in for a rude awakening if he thinks that, as the son of a rich family, he will simply (**accede, suppress**) to a position of wealth and power.

2. No doubt there are some dishonest officials, but it is a gross exaggeration to say that graft and corruption are (**rampant, explicit**) in our government.

3. Someone who insists that everyone has a price believes that human beings are (**premeditated, venal**) by nature.

4. Was Oscar Wilde being (**ironic, explicit**) when he said that he could resist everything except temptation?

5. And there was good old Dan, shouting orders, handing out papers, and generally making a(n) (**musty, officious**) nuisance of himself!

6. She may be the daughter of a factory worker, but in that evening gown she has the (**ominous, stately**) bearing of a princess.

7. His idea of debate is to shout at the top of his lungs and (**brandish, comprise**) papers with "all the facts and figures."

8. No matter how ticklish the situation, the hero always devised some (**deft, rampant**) maneuver to avoid capture.

9. Alice felt that she had reached the (**pinnacle, solace**) of fame when the principal of her former school asked for her autograph.

10. The only sure way to (**suppress, brandish**) social unrest is to make possible a decent, secure life for the people.

11. His speech at first seemed highly dramatic and impressive, but we soon realized that he was quite (**destitute, musty**) of new ideas.

12. Vivian has the kind of (**supple, stately**) personality that can easily adapt itself to a wide variety of needs and conditions.

13. They tried to "explain away" their racial slur as a slip of the tongue, but in my opinion it was deliberate and (**premeditated, ominous**).

14. Let's prepare a joint statement that will (**accede, comprise**) the various objections of all civic groups to the freeway plan.

15. Ted and I were prepared for a sharp scolding but not for the (**ominous, inopportune**) silence with which Mr. Fenno greeted us.

16. Coming at a time when I was flat broke, Molly's suggestion that we "have a bite and go to the movies" was highly (**premeditated, inopportune**).

17. Surely you can find some (**solace, pinnacle**) in the knowledge that your father had the love and respect of everyone in this community.

18. I have no patience with the (**musty, stately**) old idea that young women are not "naturally equipped" to study medicine.

19. Even in the concentration camps, some basic feelings of decency and humanity were not completely (**brandished, extirpated**).

20. If the law is intended to limit non-essential use of gasoline and heating oil, it should state this (**explicitly, ironically**).

Review   Units 4–6

Analogies   *In each of the following, encircle the item that best completes the comparison.*

1. **brandish** is to **sword** as
   a. string is to kite
   b. wave is to flag
   c. inflate is to balloon
   d. board is to airplane

2. **snob** is to **supercilious** as
   a. pauper is to venial
   b. benefactor is to malevolent
   c. thief is to nonchalant
   d. knight is to chivalrous

3. **destitute** is to **wealthy** as
   a. altruistic is to self-centered
   b. scrupulous is to meticulous
   c. supercilious is to energetic
   d. cogent is to clever

4. **invulnerable** is to **wound** as
   a. infallible is to collapse
   b. indomitable is to conquer
   c. inopportune is to risk
   d. insidious is to destroy

5. **solace** is to **grief** as
   a. wound is to bandage
   b. bequeath is to property
   c. repose is to weariness
   d. clemency is to justice

6. **infallible** is to **mistaken** as
   a. ominous is to impervious
   b. explicit is to finite
   c. scrupulous is to remiss
   d. stately is to arrogant

7. **rampant** is to **much** as
   a. opulence is to none
   b. dearth is to much
   c. destitute is to none
   d. negligible is to much

8. **malevolent** is to **unfavorable** as
   a. supple is to favorable
   b. unfeigned is to unfavorable
   c. truculent is to favorable
   d. deft is to unfavorable

9. **pinnacle** is to **high** as
   a. strait is to wide
   b. plateau is to steep
   c. ocean is to shallow
   d. abyss is to deep

10. **extirpate** is to **end** as
    a. suppress is to begin
    b. plod is to end
    c. embark is to begin
    d. comprise is to end

11. **converge** is to **together** as
    a. esteem is to below
    b. disperse is to apart
    c. assent is to above
    d. skulk is to beyond

12. **attainment** is to **achievement** as
    a. panacea is to disease
    b. clemency is to cruelty
    c. temerity is to cowardice
    d. dearth is to scarcity

13. **assent** is to **reject** as
    a. accede is to comply
    b. bequeath is to inherit
    c. ascertain is to scrutinize
    d. expunge is to erase

14. **pungent** is to **odor** as
    a. vivid is to sound
    b. musty is to appearance
    c. unkempt is to feeling
    d. spicy is to taste

15. **cogent** is to **favorable** as
    a. venal is to unfavorable
    b. officious is to favorable
    c. omniscient is to unfavorable
    d. ominous is to favorable

16. **plod** is to **quick** as
    a. trudge is to heavy
    b. sprint is to swift
    c. scamper is to slow
    d. skip is to light

17. **crime** is to **premeditated** as
    a. purpose is to prevented
    b. guilt is to presumed
    c. idea is to preconceived
    d. discrepancy is to prescribed

18. **officious** is to **meddlesome** as
    a. virulent is to harmless
    b. altruistic is to mercenary
    c. stately is to clumsy
    d. diffident is to bashful

Identification   *In each of the following groups, encircle the word that is best defined or suggested by the introductory phrase.*

1. earning a degree
a. dearth   b. assent   c. esteem   d. attainment

2. negligent of one's duty
a. diffident   b. remiss   c. omniscient   d. infallible

3. all-purpose remedy
a. panacea   b. pinnacle   c. benefactor   d. clemency

4. smooth-talking
a. cogent   b. ironic   c. facile   d. diffident

5. held in high regard
a. esteem   b. discrepancy   c. temerity   d. pinnacle

6. a shortage of supplies
a. clemency   b. dearth   c. truculence   d. solace

7. poor as a church mouse
a. altruistic   b. destitute   c. musty   d. indomitable

8. a generous patron
a. teacher   b. executive   c. counselor   d. benefactor

9. give in to the enemy's demands
a. bequeath   b. accede   c. brandish   d. comprise

10. a rattlesnake's venom
a. venial   b. virulent   c. venal   d. uncanny

11. plain and clear
a. pungent   b. explicit   c. truculent   d. ironic

12. beyond explanation
a. supercilious   b. uncanny   c. omniscient   d. infallible

13. What gall!
a. esteem   b. irony   c. temerity   d. nonchalance

14. showing good breeding
a. venal   b. supercilious   c. chivalrous   d. officious

15. like the air in a room long closed up
a. nonchalant   b. cogent   c. deft   d. musty

16. loiter suspiciously
a. skulk   b. disperse   c. plod   d. expunge

17. abounding
a. scrupulous   b. venial   c. rampant   d. nonchalant

18. drew comfort from the letters of sympathy
a. dearth   b. clemency   c. solace   d. irony

19. what one might do with a sword
a. plod   b. brandish   c. comprise   d. converge

20. carefully planned
a. premeditated   b. finite   c. uncanny   d. facile

Shades of Meaning — *Read each sentence carefully. Then encircle the item that best completes the statement below the sentence.*

History will never truly know how many lives were expunged in the intertribal holocaust that overwhelmed Rwanda in the 1990s. **(2)**

1. The word **expunged** in line 1 most nearly means
   a. affected   b. deleted   c. canceled   d. destroyed

"No one as scrupulous as she is would ever consent to be party to such an obvious piece of sharp practice," I protested. **(2)**

2. In line 1 the word **scrupulous** most nearly means
   a. religious   b. principled   c. finicky   d. knowledgeable

In his student days before World War I J.R.R. Tolkien embarked on the fantastic literary voyage that produced *The Lord of the Rings*. **(2)**

3. The words **embarked on** in line 1 most nearly mean
   a. got aboard   b. considered   c. commenced   d. wound up

At that critical moment the British Empire reposed its entire hope of safety in the abilities of a single one-armed, one-eyed sailor. **(2)**

4. In line 1 the word **reposed** most nearly means
   a. misplaced   b. gambled   c. put   d. relaxed

A foreign policy that is truly supple can both defend American interests abroad and respond successfully to unforeseen challenges. **(2)**

5. The word **supple** in line 1 is best defined as
   a. adaptable   b. superior   c. farsighted   d. bendable

Antonyms — *In each of the following groups, encircle the word or expression that is most nearly the **opposite** of the first word in **boldface type**.*

1. **deft**
   a. affiliated
   b. invulnerable
   c. remiss
   d. clumsy

2. **converge**
   a. embark
   b. assent
   c. disperse
   d. repose

3. **diffident**
   a. mild
   b. bold
   c. destitute
   d. supple

4. **nonchalant**
   a. supple
   b. embarrassed
   c. ominous
   d. ironic

5. **venial**
   a. incorruptible
   b. inexcusable
   c. indomitable
   d. unbiased

6. **attainment**
   a. failure
   b. feat
   c. repose
   d. benefactor

7. **musty**
   a. valorous
   b. explicit
   c. pungent
   d. fresh

8. **extirpate**
   a. convene
   b. imprison
   c. trust
   d. implant

9. **supercilious**	12. **unfeigned**	15. **remiss**	18. **accede**
a. untimely	a. pretended	a. altruistic	a. demur
b. dormant	b. lively	b. careless	b. brandish
c. humble	c. genuine	c. dutiful	c. suppress
d. stately	d. infallible	d. malevolent	d. bequeath
10. **ominous**	13. **cogent**	16. **omniscient**	19. **altruistic**
a. indomitable	a. stately	a. cogent	a. venial
b. favorable	b. officious	b. uncanny	b. selfish
c. deft	c. explicit	c. unfeigned	c. false
d. diffident	d. unconvincing	d. ignorant	d. remiss
11. **inopportune**	14. **plod**	17. **stately**	20. **embark**
a. uncanny	a. scamper	a. disloyal	a. suppress
b. convenient	b. assent	b. quiet	b. conclude
c. invulnerable	c. esteem	c. truculent	c. extirpate
d. cogent	d. ascertain	d. undignified	d. accede

Completing the Sentence

From the following list of words, choose the one that best completes each of the sentences below. Write the word in the appropriate space.

Group A

cogent	suppress	esteem	expunge
repose	musty	bequeath	diffident
altruistic	panacea	invulnerable	uncanny

1. Elizabeth I's _____ ability to steer a middle course in an age of fierce religious strife still astounds scholars.
2. You must learn to _____ your urge to make fun of other people if you wish to form lasting friendships.
3. All that he had to _____ to his loved ones was his good name.
4. What this _____ old office needs is fresh air and new ideas.
5. Mrs. Lobel's _____ defense of the school budget convinced many citizens that it should be approved.

Group B

clemency	converge	deft	assent
rampant	discrepancy	brandish	embark
ascertain	finite	disperse	extirpate

1. _____ a heavy stick, he raced toward me while he shouted insults and threats.
2. Delegates from all over the country _____ on the site of the national convention.

3. The mother of the convicted youth pleaded humbly with the judge to show

_____ .

4. Since our attempts to _____ our dog's breed have been fruitless, we entered her in the "mutt" category.

5. The job of the police is not to _____ the crowd but simply to keep order as long as the people wish to remain.

Word Families

A. _On the line provided, write a **noun form** of each of the following words._

EXAMPLE: embark — **embarkation**

1. stately _____
2. ironic _____
3. altruistic _____
4. pungent _____
5. ominous _____
6. bequeath _____
7. converge _____
8. disperse _____
9. suppress _____
10. affiliated _____
11. invulnerable _____
12. malevolent _____
13. chivalrous _____
14. nonchalant _____
15. omniscient _____
16. scrupulous _____
17. facile _____
18. virulent _____
19. destitute _____
20. venal _____

B. _On the line provided, write a **verb** related to each of the following words._

EXAMPLE: attainment — **attain**

1. affiliated _____
2. facile _____
3. premeditated _____
4. unfeigned _____
5. unscrupulous _____

**Filling
the Blanks**

*Encircle the pair of words that best complete the
meaning of each of the following passages.*

1. The school trustees gave up their attempt to _____ the
   identity of the donor when an intermediary explained that the mysterious
   _____ wished to remain anonymous.
   a. comprise . . . affiliation
   b. accede . . . attainment
   c. ascertain . . . benefactor
   d. esteem . . . bequest

2. While it is true that human beings are neither _____ nor
   _____ , they can certainly use what they do know to avoid
   making foolish or unnecessary mistakes.
   a. diffident . . . supercilious
   b. omniscient . . . infallible
   c. altruistic . . . malevolent
   d. indomitable . . . invulnerable

3. Pundits were quick to note the _____ when the councilman,
   who had campaigned on a reform platform, was discovered to be every bit
   as _____ as the corrupt bosses he had railed against.
   a. clemency . . . rampant
   b. discrepancy . . . venial
   c. attainment . . . altruistic
   d. irony . . . venal

4. The senator found some _____ after his electoral defeat in
   the comforting knowledge that he would now be able to enjoy a life of
   _____ , far from the strife of the political arena.
   a. esteem . . . temerity
   b. solace . . . repose
   c. panacea . . . dearth
   d. clemency . . . destitution

5. During the long years that the painter struggled to _____
   fame, his talents never failed him. However, once he had actually achieved
   the public _____ that he sought, they began to desert him.
   a. attain . . . esteem
   b. comprise . . . nonchalance
   c. suppress . . . clemency
   d. ascertain . . . pinnacle

6. 19th-century hucksters touted their "elixirs" as _____ for
   every ailment imaginable. Unfortunately, these concoctions often proved
   more _____ than the maladies they were supposed to cure.
   a. benefactors . . . musty
   b. pinnacles . . . ominous
   c. panaceas . . . virulent
   d. attainments . . . pungent

7. The salesman pressed me to sign the contract, but I refused to give my
   _____ to the agreement until all the terms and provisions he
   so vaguely mentioned were spelled out _____ .
   a. discrepancy . . . cogently
   b. esteem . . . officiously
   c. temerity . . . scrupulously
   d. assent . . . explicitly

Analogies   *In each of the following, encircle the item that best completes the comparison.*

1. cogent is to **force** as
a. opulent is to poverty
b. facile is to effort
c. urbane is to modesty
d. pungent is to bite

2. eyes are to **scrutinize** as
a. fingers are to redress
b. feet are to plod
c. ears are to brandish
d. toes are to muse

3. memory is to **expunge** as
a. artifice is to deceive
b. gibe is to extol
c. sentence is to delete
d. experiment is to retrogress

4. deft is to **adroit** as
a. inclement is to balmy
b. punitive is to punishable
c. truculent is to belligerent
d. omniscient is to infallible

5. grimace is to **pain** as
a. nod is to assent
b. yawn is to exhilaration
c. wink is to nostalgia
d. squint is to nonchalance

6. indomitable is to **overcome** as
a. infallible is to solace
b. impervious is to penetrate
c. insidious is to coerce
d. invulnerable is to heal

7. wary is to **caution** as
a. stolid is to insight
b. meticulous is to care
c. cursory is to diligence
d. tentative is to firmness

8. pliable is to **fold** as
a. remiss is to twist
b. unkempt is to comb
c. supple is to bend
d. uncanny is to explain

9. resources are to **destitute** as
a. plots are to insidious
b. bribes are to venal
c. guises are to incognito
d. relatives are to bereft

10. pinnacle is to **loom** as
a. attainment is to extend
b. chasm is to gape
c. sojourn is to embark
d. path is to converge

Shades of Meaning   *Read each sentence carefully. Then encircle the item that best completes the statement below the sentence.*

As his troops deployed, Wellington noticed a gap opening on his left flank and quickly gave orders to close it. (2)

1. In line 1 the word **deployed** most nearly means
a. prepared for a fight
b. marched briskly past
c. formed up for battle
d. stood at attention

"No matter how you cut it," Sancho Panza replied, "a chivalrous enterprise does not normally end in a joust with windmills." (2)

2. The item that best defines the word **chivalrous** in line 1 is
a. civil
b. gracious
c. courteous
d. knightly

If a piece of evidence is not cogent — that is, if it does not speak to the matter at hand — no court in the land will admit it. (2)

3. The word **cogent** is used in line 1 to mean
a. convincing
b. relevant
c. genuine
d. hearsay

As the heavens poured forth their tears, the bereft parents slowly followed
the tiny casket through the gates of the cemetery.   (2)

4. The word **bereft** in line 1 is best defined as
   a. grief-stricken through loss
   b. lacking in resources
   c. financially embarrassed
   d. deprived of strength

His only reply to my suggestion was an ironic smile that made me feel
slightly foolish and very uncomfortable.   (2)

5. The word **ironic** in line 1 most nearly means
   a. witty
   b. sarcastic
   c. remarkable
   d. poignant

Filling	*Encircle the pair of words that best complete the*
the Blanks	*meaning of each of the following sentences.*

1. In a(n) _____ gesture of reconciliation reminiscent of the
magnanimous knights of old, Abraham Lincoln declared that the Federal
government would take no _____ or retaliatory measures
against former supporters of the Confederacy.
   a. ironic . . . venial
   b. chivalrous . . . punitive
   c. craven . . . inopportune
   d. altruistic . . . tentative

2. For the umpteenth time the speaker wearily _____ her
reasons for running as an independent candidate who was in no way
_____ any organized political party in this country.
   a. ascertained . . . jeopardized by
   b. augmented . . . alienated from
   c. brandished . . . extirpated from
   d. reiterated . . . affiliated with

3. The famous chef often spoke of his truly prodigious _____
knowledge as a precious heirloom that he wished to _____
somehow to future generations of cooks all over the world.
   a. culinary . . . bequeath
   b. omniscient . . . accede
   c. opulent . . . perpetuate
   d. cursory . . . deploy

4. Though few panaceas work all the time, a trip to the barber is a(n)
_____ remedy for the great _____ of
this world.
   a. indomitable . . . unfeigned
   b. inopportune . . . uncanny
   c. infallible . . . unkempt
   d. invulnerable . . . unpremeditated

5. Most dictators eventually resort to open violence and _____
in their relentless attempts to root out resistance or _____
opposition to their regimes.
   a. nostalgia . . . harass
   b. artifice . . . adulterate
   c. quintessence . . . suppress
   d. coercion. . . . extirpate

Unit 7

Definitions

Note carefully the spelling, pronunciation, and definition of each of the following words. Then write the word in the blank space in the illustrative phrase following.

1. **abhor**
   (ab ′hôr)

   (*v.*) to regard with horror or loathing; to hate deeply

   _____ all forms of violence

2. **amend**
   (ə ′mend)

   (*v.*) to change in a formal way; to change for the better

   _____ the club's rules

3. **buffet**
   (′bəf ət)

   (*v.*) to slap or cuff; to strike repeatedly; to drive or force with blows; force one's way with difficulty; (*n.*) a slap, blow

   _____ by high winds

4. **chaos**
   (′kā äs)

   (*n.*) great confusion, disorder

   the _____ brought on by revolution

5. **commodious**
   (kə ′mō dē əs)

   (*adj.*) roomy, spacious

   a _____ pantry

6. **corrosive**
   (kə ′rō siv)

   (*adj.*) eating away gradually, acidlike; bitterly sarcastic

   angered by his _____ humor

7. **discern**
   (di ′sərn)

   (*v.*) to see clearly, recognize

   try to _____ the truth

8. **extant**
   (′ek stənt)

   (*adj.*) still existing; not exterminated, destroyed, or lost

   the oldest _____ specimens of primitive art

9. **implicate**
   (′im plə kāt)

   (*v.*) to involve in; to connect with or be related to

   _____ everyone present in the plot

10. **inter**
    (in ′tər)

    (*v.*) to bury; to consign to oblivion

    _____ those slain in battle

11. **martinet**
    (mär tə ′net)

    (*n.*) a strict disciplinarian; a stickler for the rules

    a stern _____ hated by his troops

12. **obviate**
    (′äb vē āt)

    (*v.*) to anticipate and prevent; to remove, dispose of

    took steps to _____ the difficulties

13. **renegade**
    (′ren ə gād)

    (*n.*) one who leaves a group; a deserter, outlaw; (*adj.*) traitorous; unconventional, unorthodox

    scorned by all as a _____

14. **reprehensible**
    (rep rē ′hen sə bəl)

    (*adj.*) deserving blame or punishment

    _____ acts

15. **somber**
    (′säm bər)

    (*adj.*) dark, gloomy; depressed or melancholy in spirit

    painted in dark, _____ colors

16. squalid
('skwäl id)

(*adj.*) filthy, wretched, debased

forced to live in a _____ tenement

17. turbulent
('tər byə lənt)

(*adj.*) disorderly, riotous, violent; stormy

a _____ mob of angry protesters

18. vociferous
(vō 'sif ə rəs)

(*adj.*) loud and noisy; compelling attention

_____ appeals for aid

19. voluminous
(və 'lü mə nəs)

(*adj.*) of great size; numerous; writing or speaking at great length

bored by those _____ reports

20. waive
(wāv)

(*v.*) to do without, give up voluntarily; to put off temporarily, defer

_____ their right to the property

Completing the Sentence

From the words for this unit, choose the one that best completes each of the following sentences. Write the word in the space provided.

1. Although our drill instructor went by the book, he was by no means an overbearing _____ .

2. Shakespeare tells us that "The evil that men do lives after them; the good is oft _____ with their bones."

3. In the chemistry lab, we are taught to handle all _____ substances like potash with great care.

4. The records of the School Board meetings on the proposed bond issue are so _____ that it would take me a week to read them.

5. Who would not feel depressed on entering that _____ old courtroom, with its dim lighting and dark, massive furnishings!

6. One of the signs of maturity is the ability to _____ the difference between things that are secondary and those that are truly important.

7. I didn't expect him to like my proposal, but I was shocked by his bitter and _____ criticism of it.

8. Let me say frankly that I _____ prejudice in anyone, even a member of my own family.

9. Confident that she could present the case effectively to a judge, the lawyer advised her client to _____ his right to a jury trial.

10. A person who has been _____ about by so many dreadful misfortunes will either become stronger or suffer a complete breakdown.

11. We Americans are proud that each change of the national administration, far from being _____ , is carried out in a peaceful and friendly manner.

12. In the museum we can see physical remains of many species of animals that are no longer _____ .

13. We are petitioning the council to _____ its procedures so that all citizens will have a chance to express their opinions.

14. In my innocence, I did not realize that they were "joyriding" in stolen cars, and that I would be _____ in their illegal activities.

15. Are we justified in showing visitors only the most attractive and interesting sections of our cities, towns, or villages while keeping them away from the _____ neighborhoods where so many people live?

16. The trunk of the car was so _____ that it held all of our skiing equipment as well as our other luggage.

17. A person who changes from one political party to another on the basis of honest conviction should not be regarded as a(n) _____ .

18. In our frantic search for the missing papers, we overturned everything in the room, leaving it in complete _____ .

19. The failure to vote in national elections is particularly _____ in the case of young, well-educated people.

20. You can _____ the painful need for offering apologies by not doing anything offensive in the first place.

Synonyms From the words for this unit, choose the one that is most nearly **the same** in meaning as each of the following groups of expressions. Write the word on the line provided at the right.

1. to perceive, detect, distinguish _____

2. objectionable, blameworthy, culpable; odious _____

3. to decline, relinquish, forgo _____

4. tumultuous, unruly, agitated _____

5. bulky, massive; copious, plentiful _____

6. clamorous, uproarious, blustering _____

7. caustic, mordant, acidulous; spiteful _____

8. a turncoat, defector, heretic _____

9. melancholy, mournful, dismal, gloomy _____

10. to batter, sock, thump, pummel   _____

11. dingy, sordid, foul, vile; abject   _____

12. to incriminate, entangle   _____

13. to preclude, forestall, ward off   _____

14. a taskmaster, slave driver   _____

15. surviving, existing, in existence   _____

16. to detest, despise, abominate   _____

17. comfortable, ample, capacious, roomy   _____

18. to bury, commit to the earth   _____

19. to modify; to improve, correct   _____

20. anarchy, turmoil, pandemonium   _____

Antonyms   *From the words for this unit, choose the one that is most nearly* **opposite** *in meaning to each of the following groups of expressions. Write the word on the line provided at the right.*

1. cramped, claustrophobic; insufficient   _____

2. extinct, defunct, vanished   _____

3. quiet, soft-spoken; muted, subdued   _____

4. a loyalist, patriot, unswerving adherent   _____

5. bright, sunny; lighthearted, cheerful, jaunty   _____

6. to admire, cherish, respect; to relish   _____

7. neat and clean, spruce; exalted, lofty   _____

8. to claim, accept; to insist on   _____

9. to overlook, be blind to   _____

10. scant, meager; brief, succinct   _____

11. blameless, commendable, meritorious   _____

12. to unearth, exhume   _____

13. calm, placid, tranquil, still   _____

14. order, regularity, tranquillity, peace and quiet   _____

15. to absolve, exculpate, let off the hook   _____

16. bland, mild, benign, amiable   _____

Choosing the   *Encircle the **boldface** word that more satisfactorily*
Right Word   *completes each of the following sentences.*

1. A compromise agreement reached in the judge's chambers would clearly (**discern, obviate**) the need for a long, costly lawsuit.

2. At lunchtime, the room rang with the (**reprehensible, vociferous**) debates between the Cincinnati and the Cleveland fans.

3. If you examine the evidence carefully, you will soon (**discern, amend**) the contradictions in his story.

4. The Tech team was offside on the play, but since we had thrown them for an eight-yard loss, we (**waived, abhorred**) the five-yard penalty.

5. Some people prefer the (**discernment, turbulence**) of life in a big city to the more placid atmosphere of a small town.

6. Which great poet said that his head was "bloody but unbowed" under the (**buffeting, chaos**) of fate?

7. I wouldn't say that I (**inter, abhor**) housework, but I must admit that I avoid it whenever I can.

8. Even in his old age, Thomas Jefferson kept up a (**voluminous, turbulent**) correspondence with important people in America and abroad.

9. The Founding Fathers set up a method of (**amending, obviating**) the Constitution that is neither too easy nor too difficult to use.

10. Instead of trying to help the people who had elected him, he became involved in a (**squalid, extant**) little quarrel about handing out jobs.

11. The custom by which a young man buys his bride through a payment to her father is still (**commodious, extant**) in some parts of the world.

12. History gives us many examples of how the (**vociferous, corrosive**) effects of religious hatred can weaken the entire social structure.

13. We can expect (**chaos, renegade**) in the years ahead if we do not develop a tough, realistic conservation policy.

14. When he accused me of playing fast and loose with the rules, I lost my temper and called him an officious (**renegade, martinet**).

15. Didn't it occur to them that by signing the letter "Sophomores of Central High," they would (**implicate, waive**) the entire class in the protest?

16. I don't know which was more (**somber, reprehensible**)—making improper use of the money or lying about it later.

17. I'm not so sure that I want to rent a bungalow so (**commodious, squalid**) that we'll have room for guests every weekend.

18. The time has come for us to (**implicate, inter**) our ancient disputes and go forward as a truly united people.

19. It is hard for us to realize that the great men who led our revolution were considered (**renegades, buffets**) by the British king.

20. In 1940, Winston Churchill conveyed to the British people the (**somber, voluminous**) truth that they were fighting for their national existence.

Unit 8

Note carefully the spelling, pronunciation, and definition of each of the following words. Then write the word in the blank space in the illustrative phrase following.

1. animosity
(an ə 'mäs ə tē)

(*n.*) strong dislike; bitter hostility

the growing _____ between the rival factions

2. apathy
('ap ə thē)

(*n.*) a lack of feeling, emotion, or interest

greeted my idea with total _____

3. apprehensive
(ap rē 'hen siv)

(*adj.*) fearful or anxious, especially about the future

tried to calm the _____ parents

4. commend
(kə 'mend)

(*v.*) to praise, express approval; to present as worthy of attention; to commit to the care of

_____ her for her excellent grades

5. compatible
(kəm 'pat ə bəl)

(*adj.*) able to get along or work well together; capable of use with some other model or system

statements not _____ with the facts

6. condolence
(kən 'dō ləns)

(*n.*) an expression of sympathy

a _____ call

7. consecrate
('kän sə krāt)

(*v.*) to make sacred, hallow; to set apart for a special purpose

_____ the new church

8. decrepit
(di 'krep it)

(*adj.*) old and feeble; worn-out, ruined

unwilling to ride in a _____ old car

9. deride
(de 'rīd)

(*v.*) to ridicule, laugh at with contempt

_____ our accomplishments

10. ingenuous
(in 'jen yü əs)

(*adj.*) innocent, simple; frank, sincere

take advantage of the _____ youth

11. multifarious
(məl tə 'far ē əs)

(*adj.*) having great variety; numerous and diverse

a busy schedule of _____ activities

12. obsolete
(äb sə 'lēt)

(*adj.*) out of date, no longer in use

get rid of the _____ machinery

13. omnivorous
(äm 'niv ə rəs)

(*adj.*) eating every kind of food; eagerly taking in everything, having a wide variety of tastes

an _____ animal

14. parsimonious
(pär sə 'mō nē əs)

(*adj.*) stingy, miserly; meager, poor, small

his _____ employer

15. quandary
('kwän drē)

(*n.*) a state of perplexity or doubt

help us out of this _____

16. recalcitrant
(ri 'kal sə trənt)

(*adj.*) stubbornly disobedient, resisting authority

threaten to punish the _____ children

17. reprisal
(ri 'prī zəl)

(*n.*) an injury done in return for injury

fear what they will do in _____

18. revel
('rev əl)

(*v.*) to take great pleasure in; (*n.*) a wild celebration

_____ in the attention

19. stultify
('stəl tə fī)

(*v.*) to make ineffective or useless, cripple; to have a dulling effect on

_____ by the oppressive heat

20. suave
(swäv)

(*adj.*) smoothly agreeable or polite; pleasing to the senses

a _____ man-about-town

Completing the Sentence

From the words for this unit, choose the one that best completes each of the following sentences. Write the word in the space provided.

1. I trust you will never have the experience of trying to cross the desert with a(n) _____ mule that wants to remain where it is.

2. The _____ problems facing any President in the last years of the 20th century have made his job one of the most demanding in the world.

3. If you think of all the different kinds of food that human beings are able to consume, you will realize that we are truly a(n) _____ species.

4. It is surprising how often people with very different personalities turn out to be _____ when they get to know one another.

5. This monument, said the speaker, is _____ to the memory of the men who fought and died in defense of their country.

6. If we increase our tariff rates on the goods of other countries, we can be sure that they will raise their own rates in _____ .

7. In totalitarian regimes, censorship and violence are often employed to suppress critics and _____ dissent.

8. It was difficult for us to believe that this _____ and cultured gentleman was a member of a gang of international jewel thieves.

9. Technological advances are so rapid that a particular computer may be "state-of-the-art" one day and _____ the next.

10. Throughout the hot, dusty journey, we _____ in the thought that soon we would be swimming in the cool lake.

11. So there I was, having accepted invitations to two different parties on the same evening. What a(n) _____ to be in!

12. I think that the phrase "on its last legs" is an apt description of that _____ old house down the block.

13. In spite of all the elaborate safety precautions, I couldn't help feeling _____ as she set out for her first skydiving lesson.

14. Now that I am a senior, it is hard to believe that I was ever as innocent and _____ as the members of the new freshman class.

15. Struggling to overcome his _____ inclinations, he finally reached into his pocket and handed me one thin dime!

16. Simple _____ seems to be the main reason such a large percentage of those eligible to vote fail to cast ballots in any election.

17. From all his growling and snapping, you would think our beagle felt a personal _____ toward every other dog on the block.

18. Don't you think it was in bad taste for you to _____ openly Sam's first inept attempts to dance?

19. The board of directors voted to _____ him for the skill and enthusiasm with which he had managed the charity drive.

20. Although I was unable to visit my old friend's widow in person, I offered my _____ in a heartfelt letter.

Synonyms *From the words for this unit, choose the one that is most nearly **the same** in meaning as each of the following groups of expressions. Write the word on the line provided at the right.*

1. infirm, broken-down, rickety, dilapidated _____

2. to devote, dedicate; to sanctify _____

3. naive, artless, guileless, candid _____

4. varied, manifold, heterogeneous _____

5. to praise, pat on the back; to entrust _____

6. worried, nervous, fretful, jittery _____

7. retaliation, revenge, retribution _____

8. commiseration, solace, sympathy   _____

9. sophisticated, urbane, polished   _____

10. indifference, disinterest, detachment   _____

11. frugal, niggardly, penny-pinching, "cheap"   _____

12. to smother, stifle; to neutralize, negate   _____

13. all-devouring, voracious   _____

14. to relish, savor, bask in; to carouse   _____

15. confusion; a dilemma, predicament   _____

16. unruly, obstinate, contrary, ornery   _____

17. enmity, rancor, antipathy   _____

18. outmoded, antiquated, passé, "old hat"   _____

19. to mock, scorn, disparage, jeer at   _____

20. harmonious, in agreement, like-minded   _____

Antonyms   *From the words for this unit, choose the one that is most nearly **opposite** in meaning to each of the following groups of expressions. Write the word on the line given.*

1. generous, openhanded   _____

2. to desecrate, defile, profane, dishonor   _____

3. to praise, extol, acclaim, applaud   _____

4. current, up-to-date, brand-new   _____

5. assured, confident, unworried, certain   _____

6. obedient, docile, cooperative, compliant   _____

7. artful, crafty; worldly, sophisticated   _____

8. mismatched, incongruous; antagonistic   _____

9. vigorous, robust, sturdy, hale and hearty   _____

10. unpolished, crude, clumsy, oafish, loutish   _____

11. homogeneous, uniform, unvaried   _____

12. to arouse, excite, inspire, stimulate   _____

13. affection, fondness, rapport, amity   _____

14. enthusiasm, fervor, ardor; concern   _____

15. to abhor, loathe   _____

Choosing the Right Word *Encircle the **boldface** word that more satisfactorily completes each of the following sentences.*

1. Sue is a(n) (**omnivorous, parsimonious**) reader, with a lively appetite for all types of fiction and nonfiction.

2. The address was so dull and long-winded that it seemed to (**consecrate, stultify**) rather than inspire the audience.

3. Two of the chief strengths of modern American society are the variety and vitality that arise from its (**multifarious, decrepit**) cultures.

4. When Meg appeared with a stack of record albums, we realized that our crash study session might become an all-day (**reprisal, revel**).

5. Your unwillingness to study foreign languages is in no way (**compatible, omnivorous**) with your ambition to get a job in the Foreign Service.

6. I must give you the sad news that correct spelling and good grammar are not, and will never be, (**obsolete, decrepit**).

7. The diplomat was so (**suave, ingenuous**) and self-assured in his manner that we took him for a headwaiter.

8. Yes, there is some (**animosity, apathy**) between different racial and ethnic groups, but it can be overcome by education and experience.

9. Those students who have been doing their work all term need not feel (**apprehensive, recalcitrant**) about the final examination.

10. The handful of (**recalcitrant, parsimonious**) students who refuse to obey study hall regulations are violating the rights of the majority.

11. So we are faced with that old (**quandary, reprisal**)—an income that simply can't be stretched to cover the things that we simply must have.

12. If you can't (**deride, commend**) me for my efforts to help you, at least don't criticize me for not doing everything you want.

13. I think we should offer congratulations, rather than (**revels, condolences**), for the disappearance of that battered old heap you called a car.

14. Her moods seem to go from one extreme to the other—from deepest (**apathy, animosity**) to unlimited enthusiasm.

15. He is so absorbed in himself that he has become (**parsimonious, suave**) in the normal expression of human sympathy and affection.

16. As we begin the third century of our nation's life, we should (**commend, consecrate**) ourselves anew to the ideals of human freedom.

17. Although our society must punish criminals, I don't think we should do so simply as a (**reprisal, quandary**) for the wrongs they have committed.

18. Obviously jealous of Peter's fine talk before the school assembly, Dan tried to (**revel, deride**) him as "the boy orator of East 7th Street."

19. Can you be so (**parsimonious, ingenuous**) that you don't realize she is paying us all those phony compliments to get something out of us?

20. Our Constitution is 200 years old, but far from being (**suave, decrepit**), it is still a vital, dynamic, and highly practical plan of government.

Unit 9

Definitions

Note carefully the spelling, pronunciation, and definition of each of the following words. Then write the word in the blank space in the illustrative phrase following.

1. **allocate**
   ('al ə kāt)

   (*v.*) to set apart or designate for a special purpose; to distribute

   _____ funds for the project

2. **ardent**
   ('är dənt)

   (*adj.*) very enthusiastic, impassioned

   the joy of an _____ fisherman

3. **assiduous**
   (ə 'sij ü əs)

   (*adj.*) persistent, attentive, diligent

   an _____ student

4. **brash**
   (brash)

   (*adj.*) prone to act in a hasty manner; impudent

   a _____ young hothead

5. **capricious**
   (kə 'prish əs)

   (*adj.*) subject to whims or passing fancies

   confused by his _____ behavior

6. **chastise**
   (chas 'tīz)

   (*v.*) to inflict physical punishment as a means of correction; to scold severely

   _____ the careless employees

7. **copious**
   ('kō pē əs)

   (*adj.*) abundant; plentiful; wordy, verbose

   take _____ notes

8. **deviate**
   (*v.*, 'dē vē āt;
   n., adj., 'dē vē ət)

   (*v.*) to turn aside; to stray from a norm; (*n.*) one who departs from a norm; (*adj.*) differing from a norm, heterodox, unconventional

   _____ from the original plan

9. **emaciated**
   (i 'mā shē ā tid)

   (*adj., part.*) made unnaturally thin

   the starving man's _____ body

10. **exult**
    (eg 'zəlt)

    (*v.*) to rejoice greatly

    _____ in their unexpected victory

11. **gnarled**
    (närld)

    (*adj.*) knotted, twisted, lumpy

    the _____ limbs of the old oak tree

12. **indemnity**
    (in 'dem nə tē)

    (*n.*) a payment for damage or loss

    demand some _____ for his losses

13. **inkling**
    ('iŋk liŋ)

    (*n.*) a hint; a vague notion

    gave no _____ of how she really felt

14. **limpid**
    ('lim pid)

    (*adj.*) clear, transparent; readily understood

    the _____ waters of a mountain lake

15. **omnipotent**
    (äm 'nip ə tənt)

    (*adj.*) almighty, having unlimited power or authority

    do not want an _____ ruler

16. palatable
('pal ə tə bəl)

(*adj.*) agreeable to the taste or one's sensibilities; suitable for consumption

find the food most _____

17. poignant
('poin yənt)

(*adj.*) deeply affecting, touching; keen or sharp in taste or smell

a _____ death scene

18. rancor
('raŋ kər)

(*n.*) bitter resentment or ill-will

felt no _____ at his defeat

19. sophomoric
(säf ə 'môr ik)

(*adj.*) immature but overconfident; conceited

vexed by their _____ comments

20. spontaneous
(spän 'tā nē əs)

(*adj.*) arising naturally; not planned or engineered in advance

the _____ reaction of a child

Completing the Sentence

From the words for this unit, choose the one that best completes each of the following sentences. Write the word in the space provided.

1. Remembering Fred as a robust 200-pounder, I was shocked to see how _____ he had become during his long illness.

2. _____ is never so bitter as when it arises among people who were once close friends.

3. Aunt Cora arrived with nine pieces of luggage, assorted medical equipment, and _____ supplies of good advice.

4. My travels have shown me that many exotic foods I once considered "disgusting" are really quite _____ .

5. How can you say that the audience's reaction was _____ when the director held up a sign reading "Applause"?

6. When he told me that he was reading *Huckleberry Finn* for the ninth time, I realized that he was indeed a(n) _____ admirer of the novel.

7. Somewhere in a(n) _____ pool in the Canadian Rockies is the large trout that will someday grace the wall of my den.

8. If you were as _____ in studying foreign affairs as you are in memorizing batting averages, you would have known how to reply to his comments on the situation in the Middle East.

9. Nothing can arouse _____ memories of long ago and faraway like an old, well-loved song!

10. The teacher decided to _____ a corner of the classroom to an exhibition of student science projects.

11. We were fascinated to see the consummate grace and skill with which the _____ hands of the old carpenter manipulated his tools.

12. Wasn't it rather _____ of Frank to offer the football coach some "advice" on his very first day as a candidate for the team?

13. Some of my friends are mentally rather mature for their age; others are of a decidedly _____ turn of mind.

14. Her casting decisions for the class play are _____ , with no real attempt to select the people best suited for the roles.

15. As the speaker's voice droned on endlessly in the hot, crowded room, I suddenly realized that I hadn't the slightest _____ of what he was saying.

16. The Bible tells us that the Lord will _____ the wicked, but our Student Dean is trying very hard to help Him out.

17. If you wish to recover quickly, you must not _____ in the slightest from the doctor's instructions.

18. Under the American system of separation of powers, no government official or agency can ever become _____ .

19. There can be no _____ for the pain and suffering that your carelessness has caused me!

20. General Grant accepted Lee's surrender with quiet dignity, refusing to _____ over the defeat of a worthy foe.

Synonyms From the words for this unit, choose the one that is most nearly **the same** in meaning as each of the following groups of expressions. Write the word on the line given.

1. ample, profuse, bountiful _____

2. gaunt, withered, shriveled, all skin and bones _____

3. a clue, intimation, suggestion _____

4. edible; appetizing, attractive _____

5. compensation, restitution, reparation _____

6. all-powerful _____

7. unpremeditated, unplanned, impromptu _____

8. heartrending, bittersweet, melancholy _____

9. to diverge, veer, swerve _____

10. lucid, intelligible; transparent, clear _____

11. rash, impetuous; brazen, impertinent _____

12. knotty, misshapen, contorted _____

13. industrious, unremitting, sedulous _____

14. animosity, enmity, bitterness _____

15. pretentious; superficial, fatuous _____

16. to assign, allot, apportion _____

17. to rejoice, revel, glory in _____

18. to discipline, censure, call on the carpet _____

19. intense, zealous, fervent, avid _____

20. impulsive, fickle, unpredictable, mercurial _____

Antonyms   *From the words for this unit, choose the one that is most nearly **opposite** in meaning to each of the following groups of expressions. Write the word on the line given.*

1. to commend, pat on the back; to reward _____

2. unaffecting, bland, vapid, insipid; funny _____

3. clouded, murky; opaque _____

4. powerless, impotent, feeble, weak _____

5. smooth, unblemished; straight _____

6. to conform to, abide by; orthodox _____

7. inedible; distasteful, disagreeable _____

8. planned, contrived, premeditated, rehearsed _____

9. to mope, sulk; to regret, rue, lament _____

10. mature; judicious, sage; knowledgeable _____

11. goodwill, harmony, rapport, amity _____

12. constant, steady, steadfast, unwavering _____

13. indifferent, stolid, phlegmatic, apathetic _____

14. plump, fat, obese, corpulent _____

15. inadequate; meager, scanty; concise _____

16. prudent, wary, cautious, circumspect _____

17. lazy, lackadaisical, shiftless _____

68

Choosing the Right Word

*Encircle the **boldface** word that more satisfactorily completes each of the following sentences.*

1. Paul tries to sound well-informed, but his pretentious answers only betray his (**poignant, sophomoric**) knowledge of world affairs.

2. Our meeting last week was marred by a heated debate over how to (**allocate, chastise**) the funds in this year's budget.

3. In the concentration camps, the liberating troops found thousands of victims horribly (**capricious, emaciated**) as the result of starvation diets.

4. Sylvia was (**assiduous, brash**) enough to tell her mother she was going to the dance in spite of the doctor's orders.

5. Since their loud talk and crude manners were anything but (**palatable, limpid**) to me, I decided to travel by myself.

6. Her (**ardent, brash**) interest in ecology shows that she cares deeply about the welfare of this planet.

7. The tastes of the TV audience are so (**gnarled, capricious**) that no one can predict in advance which programs will be successful.

8. Perhaps you have been treated unfairly, but what good will it do to allow your sense of (**indemnity, rancor**) to control your mood and behavior?

9. He seems to feel that it is his mission in life to (**exult, chastise**) all those who fail to live up to his standards.

10. The lecturer explained that the UN is not (**palatable, omnipotent**) and that it can do only what the member states allow it to do.

11. What he lacks in skill, he makes up in (**assiduous, spontaneous**) attention to every last detail and requirement of the job.

12. During the depression of the 1930s, the entire nation seemed to take new strength from Roosevelt's (**poignant, copious**) energy and enthusiasm.

13. George Gershwin's early songs gave only a dim (**inkling, deviation**) of the genius that was to express itself in *Porgy and Bess*.

14. After so many years of losing teams, the entire student body (**exulted, gnarled**) when our team finally won the citywide basketball championship.

15. Her simple, (**spontaneous, capricious**) expression of appreciation meant more to me than all the elaborate, carefully phrased tributes I received.

16. The destruction wrought by a nuclear war would be so vast that any form of (**indemnity, inkling**) to the injured would be impossible.

17. We must show understanding and acceptance of those who (**deviate, exult**) somewhat from our own standards of what is "right."

18. Far from being "effortless," her simple, (**limpid, capricious**) writing style is the result of the most painstaking efforts.

19. His weatherbeaten, shaggy, and (**gnarled, assiduous**) appearance did not conceal entirely traces of the handsome boy I had once known.

20. Tennyson speaks of "sorrow's crown of sorrow," by which he means the (**poignant, copious**) experience of remembering happier things.

Analogies *In each of the following, encircle the item that best completes the comparison.*

1. omnipotent is to **power** as
a. omnivorous is to appetite
b. ominous is to wisdom
c. omniscient is to knowledge
d. omnipresent is to skill

2. thin is to **emaciated** as
a. ingenuous is to dishonest
b. mercenary is to compatible
c. decrepit is to sickly
d. tired is to exhausted

3. suave is to **boorish** as
a. turbulent is to peaceful
b. voluminous is to copious
c. capricious is to brash
d. limpid is to transparent

4. assiduous is to **favorable** as
a. palatable is to unfavorable
b. recalcitrant is to favorable
c. reprehensible is to unfavorable
d. squalid is to favorable

5. palatable is to **taste** as
a. gnarled is to texture
b. vociferous is to appearance
c. commodious is to sound
d. brash is to sight

6. indemnity is to **loss** as
a. condolence is to sympathy
b. reprisal is to injury
c. apathy is to triumph
d. rancor is to spite

7. chastise is to **commend** as
a. deviate is to veer
b. amend is to deride
c. inter is to consecrate
d. abhor is to relish

8. decrepit is to **vigor** as
a. apprehensive is to confidence
b. recalcitrant is to obstinacy
c. parsimonious is to thrift
d. ingenuous is to ignorance

9. stultify is to **stifle** as
a. allocate is to waive
b. obviate is to commend
c. consecrate is to profane
d. implicate is to incriminate

10. ardent is to **apathy** as
a. apprehensive is to anxiety
b. brash is to audacity
c. somber is to levity
d. suave is to polish

11. inkling is to **intimation** as
a. buffet is to quandary
b. condolence is to animosity
c. rancor is to resentment
d. chaos is to indemnity

12. extant is to **extinct** as
a. chaotic is to orderly
b. poignant is to sad
c. spontaneous is to obsolete
d. somber is to corrosive

13. exult is to **triumphant** as
a. inter is to vociferous
b. despair is to vanquished
c. spend is to parsimonious
d. obey is to recalcitrant

14. pool is to **limpid** as
a. explanation is to lucid
b. quandary is to compatible
c. combustion is to spontaneous
d. apathy is to assiduous

15. copious is to **quantity** as
a. multifarious is to duration
b. vociferous is to range
c. commodious is to capacity
d. voluminous is to application

16. vengeful is to **reprisals** as
a. timid is to quandaries
b. contrite is to amends
c. somber is to revels
d. callous is to condolences

17. martinet is to **discipline** as
a. renegade is to loyalty
b. miser is to poverty
c. scholar is to ignorance
d. aesthete is to beauty

18. quandary is to **perplex** as
a. deviation is to conform
b. riddle is to stump
c. dilemma is to solve
d. predicament is to escape

Identification *In each of the following groups, encircle the word that is best defined or suggested by the introductory phrase.*

1. said of an act that is done hastily, without regard for consequences
a. ardent   b. corrosive   c. brash   d. turbulent

2. state of uncertainty or puzzlement
a. condolence   b. apathy   c. rancor   d. quandary

3. feeling of ill-will or resentment
a. indemnity   b. animosity   c. reprisal   d. buffet

4. noisy celebration
a. allocation   b. revel   c. consecration   d. deviate

5. state of complete disorder
a. reprisal   b. waive   c. rancor   d. chaos

6. avoid the necessity for doing something
a. obviate   b. inter   c. chastise   d. discern

7. said of a lawn mower that is difficult to start
a. compatible   b. recalcitrant   c. somber   d. ardent

8. make an addition or improvement
a. allocate   b. inkling   c. reprisal   d. amend

9. economical to the point of stinginess
a. apprehensive   b. suave   c. parsimonious   d. ingenuous

10. out-of-date
a. gnarled   b. reprehensible   c. turbulent   d. obsolete

11. numerous and diverse
a. assiduous   b. multifarious   c. poignant   d. extant

12. an expression of sympathy
a. indemnity   b. reprisal   c. condolence   d. inkling

13. straying from the straight and narrow
a. deviate   b. ingenuous   c. ardent   d. spontaneous

14. how one might describe the limbs of an oak tree
a. omnivorous   b. somber   c. limpid   d. gnarled

15. lay to rest
a. stultify   b. obviate   c. deviate   d. inter

16. on its last legs
a. capricious   b. decrepit   c. gnarled   d. renegade

17. divvy up the chores
a. implicate   b. waive   c. allocate   d. deride

18. on the spur of the moment
a. spontaneous   b. reprehensible   c. extant   d. turbulent

19. all skin and bones
a. suave   b. corrosive   c. emaciated   d. squalid

20. said of a "tearjerker"
a. capricious   b. ingenuous   c. multifarious   d. poignant

Shades of Meaning

Read each sentence carefully. Then encircle the item that best completes the statement below the sentence.

I was in the midst of the usual explanation of the poem when a renegade thought crossed my mind and stopped me dead in my tracks. **(2)**

1. In line 1 the word **renegade** is best defined as
a. brilliant
b. unorthodox
c. unworthy
d. outlawed

Let us waive judgment until all the facts of the matter are in and we can better assess the merits of the case. **(2)**

2. The word **waive** in line 1 is best defined as
a. relinquish permanently
b. refuse absolutely
c. postpone temporarily
d. rush hastily to

"O Lord," the chaplain said softly, "we commend the body of our fallen comrade to the deep and his soul to thy eternal care." **(2)**

3. In line 1 the word **commend** is used to mean
a. praise
b. entrust
c. approve
d. surrender

Unfortunately, the software program I wanted was not compatible with the brand of personal computer I had bought. **(2)**

4. The word **compatible** in line 1 most nearly means
a. usable
b. sympathetic
c. cooperative
d. harmonious

Listening to overblown soapbox oratory has made me appreciate just how apt Dr. Johnson's phrase "copious without order" still is. **(2)**

5. The word **copious** in line 2 is best defined as
a. generous
b. abounding
c. disorganized
d. wordy

Antonyms

*In each of the following groups, encircle the word or expression that is most nearly the **opposite** of the first word in **boldface type**.*

1. capricious
a. unselfish
b. steady
c. impulsive
d. limpid

2. deride
a. ridicule
b. discern
c. praise
d. waive

3. squalid
a. decrepit
b. opulent
c. poignant
d. intense

4. apprehensive
a. confident
b. uncertain
c. cautious
d. understanding

5. assiduous
a. compatible
b. lazy
c. somber
d. chaotic

6. copious
a. plentiful
b. squalid
c. in short supply
d. well-planned

7. waive
a. claim
b. reject
c. brandish
d. buffet

8. suave
a. spontaneous
b. multifarious
c. omnipotent
d. crude

9. **implicate**	12. **abhor**	15. **animosity**	18. **commend**
a. fold	a. love	a. rancor	a. donate
b. complicate	b. despise	b. derision	b. repair
c. find guilty	c. punish	c. affection	c. separate
d. absolve	d. exult	d. weariness	d. scold
10. **vociferous**	13. **consecrate**	16. **stultify**	19. **extant**
a. convincing	a. obviate	a. excite	a. defunct
b. energetic	b. amend	b. chatter	b. recalcitrant
c. soft-spoken	c. precede	c. inter	c. gnarled
d. eloquent	d. profane	d. cooperate	d. omnipotent
11. **limpid**	14. **commodious**	17. **reprehensible**	20. **ardent**
a. clouded	a. out of tune	a. blameless	a. brash
b. gnarled	b. cramped	b. renegade	b. chaotic
c. emaciated	c. agreeable	c. uncaptured	c. indifferent
d. squalid	d. voluminous	d. implicated	d. turbulent

Completing the Sentence *From the following list of words, choose the one that best completes each of the sentences below. Write the word in the appropriate space.*

Group A

extant	decrepit	squalid	revel
implicate	obviate	corrosive	sophomoric
martinet	renegade	commodious	discern

1. Her wit was so biting and her criticism so penetrating that a reviewer aptly described her book as _____ .

2. In later life he became a _____ whose obsession with rules and regulations became proverbial.

3. Dismissing my answer as pretentious and superficial, the teacher warned me not to vex her with such _____ nonsense again.

4. It was hard for us to believe that this _____ old man was a former Olympic hurdling champion.

5. Red Cross officials were appalled by the _____ conditions they found in the makeshift refugee camp.

Group B

indemnity	consecrate	amend	quandary
deride	exult	vociferous	waive
inter	chastise	capricious	buffet

1. Our society needs people who will _____ themselves to the service of humanity.

2. How long can you expect me to sit by in silence while you continue to _____ things that I admire and respect!

3. The only way out of your _____ is to admit that you were wrong and to do all you can to make up for your faults.

4. We never know what to expect from a person whose moods are so

_____ .

5. Our hopes for financial independence were _____ in the wreckage of the bankrupt firm in which we had invested so heavily.

Word Families

A. On the line provided, write a **noun form** of each of the following words.

EXAMPLE: assiduous—**assiduousness**

1. spontaneous _____
2. compatible _____
3. squalid _____
4. brash _____
5. consecrate _____
6. poignant _____
7. turbulent _____
8. amend _____
9. apprehensive _____
10. discern _____
11. abhor _____
12. inter _____
13. capricious _____
14. implicate _____
15. commend _____
16. chastise _____
17. deviate _____
18. exult _____
19. corrosive _____

B. On the line provided, write a **verb** related to each of the following words.

EXAMPLE: commodious—**accommodate**

1. corrosive _____
2. indemnity _____
3. condolence _____
4. renegade _____
5. gnarled _____

**Filling
the Blanks**

*Encircle the pair of words that best complete the
meaning of each of the following passages.*

1. The soldiers who fell in the engagement were _____ in a
portion of the battlefield on which they had fought. The spot where they
were laid to rest was not technically "hallowed ground." Still, it was
considered appropriate because they had in effect _____
it with their blood.

   a. discerned . . . commended   c. interred . . . consecrated
   b. chastised . . . waived   d. implicated . . . buffeted

2. Though I am perfectly willing to give praise where I feel praise is due, I
refuse to _____ an action that I consider underhanded and

_____ .

   a. abhor . . . extant   c. deride . . . sophomoric
   b. commend . . . reprehensible   d. amend . . . apprehensive

3. As the storm increased in intensity, the normally calm waters of the lake
became more and more _____ . Strong gusts of wind
slapped at our sails, and our tiny craft was _____ about
like a Ping-Pong ball in an electric blender.

   a. turbulent . . . buffeted   c. vociferous . . . waived
   b. voluminous . . . deviated   d. capricious . . . derided

4. I hoped that my project proposal would be hailed by my classmates with
_____ enthusiasm. Instead, it was greeted with "deafening"

_____ .

   a. sophomoric . . . indemnity   c. vociferous . . . apathy
   b. compatible . . . animosity   d. copious . . . chaos

5. "My years of foreign service have taught me to be as _____
as possible," the veteran diplomat observed, his tongue firmly in his cheek.
"These days, turning up one's nose at another country's national dish, no
matter how _____ , might just trigger a very unpleasant
international incident."

   a. recalcitrant . . . disingenuous   c. compatible . . . squalid
   b. suave . . . chaotic   d. omnivorous . . . unpalatable

6. Infuriated by their treacherous behavior, the enraged party leader severely
_____ the _____ who had unexpectedly
bolted to the opposition during the crucial vote.

   a. chastised . . . renegades   c. implicated . . . martinets
   b. consecrated . . . deviates   d. derided . . . revelers

Analogies *In each of the following, encircle the item that best completes the comparison.*

1. brash is to **temerity** as
a. fervent is to apathy
b. chivalrous is to artifice
c. hard-hearted is to clemency
d. ardent is to enthusiasm

2. omniscient is to **know** as
a. omnipotent is to subject
b. infallible is to think
c. omnivorous is to eat
d. invulnerable is to wound

3. negligible is to **little** as
a. bereft is to much
b. commodious is to little
c. copious is to much
d. rampant is to little

4. shanty is to **squalid** as
a. bungalow is to stately
b. palace is to opulent
c. cottage is to decrepit
d. condominium is to obsolete

5. recalcitrant is to **mule** as
a. stolid is to cow
b. ironic is to weasel
c. supercilious is to pig
d. ingenuous is to sheep

6. somber is to **mood** as
a. ambidextrous is to temperament
b. facile is to effort
c. vociferous is to noise
d. dour is to disposition

7. abhor is to **esteem** as
a. attire is to redress
b. chastise is to commend
c. delete is to excise
d. implicate is to suppress

8. gibes are to **deride** as
a. panaceas are to injure
b. mistakes are to amend
c. condolences are to solace
d. attainments are to obviate

9. corrosive is to **burn** as
a. poignant is to pinch
b. limpid is to bite
c. cogent is to scratch
d. pungent is to sting

10. skinflint is to **parsimonious** as
a. busybody is to officious
b. renegade is to loyal
c. craven is to emaciated
d. deviate is to capricious

Shades of Meaning *Read each sentence carefully. Then encircle the item that best completes the statement below the sentence.*

Slowly but surely the grand old frigate buffeted its way through the turbulent seas off that storm-tossed coast. **(2)**

1. The word **buffeted** in line 1 is best defined as
a. threaded
b. pushed
c. sought
d. pummeled

The book claims to be an "impartial analysis of the issue," but its unkempt prose shows it to be the work of a fanatic. **(2)**

2. In line 1 the word **unkempt** most nearly means
a. uncombed
b. lucid
c. wordy
d. sloppy

It is horrifying to think that 130 years after the war, so many of the animosities that produced it have still not been interred. **(2)**

3. The word **interred** in line 2 is best defined as
a. consigned to the earth
b. laid to rest
c. put on the back burner
d. engraved in our hearts

Our tradition of academic freedom allows all views, orthodox and deviate alike, to be heard unmolested.

(2)

4. The word **deviate** in line 1 is best defined as
   a. straying
   b. commonplace
   c. unconventional
   d. substandard

Facile solutions to complex problems do not impress me, nor do those who forward such ideas to attain their own ends.

(2)

5. In line 1 the word **Facile** most nearly means
   a. Spurious
   b. Modest
   c. Weird
   d. Fluent

**Filling
the Blanks**

Encircle the pair of words that best complete the meaning of each of the following sentences.

1. In a truly eerie opening scene, the _____ sight of the ghost of Hamlet's father walking on the battlements fills three very superstitious mortals with fear and _____ .
   a. poignant . . . animosity
   b. ominous . . . temerity
   c. somber . . . nostalgia
   d. uncanny . . . apprehension

2. Though I love to _____ in a friend's success, I have never been able to take delight in the discomfiture of a(n) _____ .
   a. revel . . . adversary
   b. accede . . . martinet
   c. converge . . . craven
   d. exult . . . benefactor

3. The _____ old house, a hoary relic of a bygone era, had been closed up for so many years that a(n) _____ odor permeated the atmosphere of every room like an evil yellow fog.
   a. stately . . . tepid
   b. malevolent . . . suave
   c. decrepit . . . musty
   d. squalid . . . limpid

4. It was one of life's little _____ that the implacable judge who had so _____ condemned others to the gallows should himself die by the noose.
   a. quandaries . . . scrupulously
   b. ironies . . . assiduously
   c. discrepancies . . . meticulously
   d. artifices . . . warily

5. In his will, the philanthropist _____ a sizable portion of his great fortune to such _____ endeavors as sheltering the homeless and feeding the hungry.
   a. allocated . . . altruistic
   b. deployed . . . virulent
   c. commended . . . diffident
   d. consecrated . . . obsolete

Unit 10

Definitions

Note carefully the spelling, pronunciation, and definition of each of the following words. Then write the word in the blank space in the illustrative phrase following.

1. acquiesce
(ak wē 'es)

(*v.*) to accept without protest; to agree or submit

_____ to their demands

2. allure
(a 'lür)

(*v.*) to entice, tempt; to be attractive to; (*n.*) a strong attraction; the power to attract, charm

_____ with promises of great wealth

3. askew
(ə 'skyü)

(*adj., adv.*) twisted to one side, crooked; disapprovingly

with his tie all _____

4. blithe
(blīth)

(*adj.*) cheerful, lighthearted; casual, unconcerned

the _____ optimism of youth

5. contentious
(kən 'ten shəs)

(*adj.*) quarrelsome, inclined to argue

annoyed by his _____ manner

6. covet
('kəv ət)

(*v.*) to desire something belonging to another

_____ his videocassette collection

7. crestfallen
('krest fô lən)

(*adj.*) discouraged, dejected, downcast

comfort the _____ losers

8. disheveled
(di 'shev əld)

(*adj.*) rumpled, mussed; hanging in disorder

always seemed to be untidy and _____

9. exponent
(ek 'spō nənt)

(*n.*) one who advocates, speaks for, explains, or interprets; (*math*) the power to which a number, symbol, or expression is to be raised; (*adj.*) explanatory

an ardent _____ of modern art

10. garrulous
('gar ə ləs)

(*adj.*) given to much talking, tediously chatty

impatient with the _____ old woman

11. insuperable
(in 'sü pər ə bəl)

(*adj.*) incapable of being overcome

an _____ obstacle to success

12. lamentable
('lam ən tə bəl)

(*adj.*) to be regretted or pitied

victim of a _____ accident

13. misnomer
(mis 'nō mər)

(*n.*) an unsuitable or misapplied name

felt that the title was a _____

14. profess
(prə 'fes)

(*v.*) to affirm openly; to state belief in; to claim, pretend

_____ satisfaction in our work

15. respite
('res pit)

(*n.*) a period of relief and rest

seek _____ from worry

16. retribution
(re trə ′byü shən)

(*n.*) a repayment; a deserved punishment

suffered _____ for his crimes

17. sinuous
(′sin yü əs)

(*adj.*) winding, having many curves; lithe and flexible

the dancer's _____ movements

18. sonorous
(′sə nôr əs)

(*adj.*) **full, deep, or rich in sound; impressive in style**

soothed by the _____ music

19. vanguard
(′van gärd)

(*n.*) the foremost part of an army; the leading position in any field

be in the _____ of progress

20. wastrel
(′wās trəl)

(*n.*) a wasteful person, spendthrift; a good-for-nothing

the self-destructive life of a _____

Completing the Sentence

From the words for this unit, choose the one that best completes each of the following sentences. Write the word in the space provided.

1. Driving a car along those _____ mountain roads at a height of 10,000 feet calls for stronger nerves than I have.

2. After I heard my new canary sing, I decided that "Melody," the name I had planned for it, was something of a _____ .

3. In spite of her rain-soaked clothing and _____ appearance, it seemed to me that she had never looked lovelier.

4. After all my high hopes, I was utterly _____ when the notice arrived that I had failed the driver's test.

5. The _____ personality that had made her so charming and popular was unaffected by the passage of the years.

6. I confess I suffered a twinge of envy when I learned that my rival had won the prize I had _____ so dearly.

7. He says that he is spending the family fortune "to promote the art of good living," but I consider him no more than a(n) _____ .

8. A staunch believer in the equality of the sexes, Susan B. Anthony was one of the most effective _____ of women's rights.

9. Retailers who seek to _____ unwary consumers with false claims should feel the full penalties of the law.

10. Now that the football season has ended, don't you think our athletes deserve a brief _____ before beginning basketball practice?

11. We can all agree that the crime situation in this community is truly _____ , but what are we going to do about it?

12. The body of the slain hero was accompanied to its final resting place by the _____ strains of a funeral march.

13. It isn't likely that the school administration will _____ to your recommendation to do away with all examinations and grades.

14. With the publication of her famous book _Silent Spring_, Rachel Carson moved into the _____ of those seeking to protect our natural environment.

15. You certainly have a right to your opinions, but you have become so _____ that you immediately challenge opinions expressed by anyone else.

16. The pioneers succeeded in settling the West because they refused to admit that any obstacle, however formidable, was _____ .

17. For the innumerable crimes and cruelties he had committed, the tyrant had good reason to fear human, if not divine, _____ .

18. Excessively _____ people don't have the imagination to realize that their endless chatter is boring everyone else.

19. I do not _____ to be heroic, but I hope I have the nerve to stand up for unpopular ideas that I believe are right.

20. If you had listened more carefully to the instructions on operating the sewing machine, the seams would not have gone _____ .

Synonyms From the words for this unit, choose the one that is most nearly **the same** in meaning as each of the following groups of expressions. Write the word on the line provided at the right.

1. argumentative, disputatious, combative _____

2. untidy, disarranged, tousled, unkempt _____

3. deplorable, regrettable, distressing _____

4. recompense, requital, just deserts _____

5. resonant, resounding; grandiloquent _____

6. awry, lopsided, cockeyed _____

7. to assert, declare, proclaim; to purport _____

8. to yearn for, hunger for, crave _____

9. despondent, disconsolate _____

10. a loafer, idler; a squanderer, profligate _____

11. invincible, insurmountable, indomitable   _____

12. temptation, enticement; to beguile tantalize   _____

13. the forefront, cutting edge; trailblazers   _____

14. a defender, champion; an interpreter   _____

15. twisting, convoluted, serpentine; supple   _____

16. an interval, intermission, lull, "breather"   _____

17. to comply, accede, consent, yield   _____

18. talkative, loquacious, long-winded   _____

19. carefree, nonchalant, indifferent   _____

20. a misnaming, malapropism   _____

Antonyms   *From the words for this unit, choose the one that is most nearly **opposite** in meaning to each of the following groups of expressions. Write the word on the line provided at the right.*

1. neat, tidy, orderly, well-groomed   _____

2. surmountable, conquerable   _____

3. elated, cheerful; self-satisfied, cocky   _____

4. tinny, reedy, harsh and grating   _____

5. direct, straight, unbending; stiff, rigid   _____

6. agreeable, amiable, affable; pacific   _____

7. to disclaim, disavow, repudiate   _____

8. to repel, turn off; a repellent   _____

9. a skinflint, tightwad, miser   _____

10. the rearguard; stragglers, laggards   _____

11. a critic, adversary, faultfinder, detractor   _____

12. reticent, mum, taciturn, laconic, reserved   _____

13. praiseworthy, commendable, laudable   _____

14. straight, symmetrical   _____

15. to resist, protest, drag one's heels   _____

16. glum, morose, despondent, depressed   _____

17. to disdain, scorn, despise   _____

Choosing the Right Word   *Encircle the **boldface** word that more satisfactorily completes each of the following sentences.*

1. His willingness to experiment with interesting new ideas clearly put him in the (**vanguard, retribution**) of social reform in his time.

2. The taxi driver was so (**lamentable, garrulous**) during the long trip that it was a relief to return to my lonely hotel room.

3. Since it was the duty of town criers to deliver public proclamations, they were often chosen for their (**sonorous, contentious**) voices.

4. Since Ben was confident he could play varsity ball, he was extremely (**blithe, crestfallen**) when the coach cut him from the squad.

5. Anyone who spends hours, days, and weeks just "hanging around" is a (**wastrel, vanguard**) with the most precious thing we have—*time*.

6. After we had been playing our best rock records for several hours, mother entered the room and begged for some (**respite, allure**).

7. Although we really don't agree with mother's musical tastes, we decided to (**respite, acquiesce**) to her appeal.

8. The poet Shelley, entranced by the joyous song of the skylark, addressed the bird as "(**garrulous, blithe**) spirit."

9. As I watched the gymnastic meet on TV, nothing impressed me more than the incredibly graceful and (**askew, sinuous**) movements of the athletes.

10. The intently longing gaze that he fixed upon my plate told me that Rover (**professed, coveted**) my lunch.

11. Wasteful use of energy at a time when there is a critical shortage of such resources is indeed (**lamentable, sonorous**).

12. (**Crestfallen, Allured**) by the breathtaking views that appeared as we climbed, we struggled our way to the top ledge of Mount Potash.

13. It would be a (**misnomer, respite**) to label as biography a book that is clearly a work of fiction, even though its main character is historical.

14. With present-day hair styles what they are, many men now seem to look somewhat (**disheveled, garrulous**) when they come fresh from the barber.

15. Walking out on the empty stage and speaking the opening lines of the play seemed an (**covetous, insuperable**) difficulty to the young actors.

16. Cy is so (**contentious, sinuous**) that if someone says "Nice day," he'll start a full-scale debate on the weather.

17. When we ended up in the lake, we realized that Ralph was not the expert boatman he (**acquiesced, professed**) to be.

18. The wicked may seem to prosper, but I am convinced that sometime, somehow, in this life or the next, there will be (**exponents, retribution**).

19. With her lipstick smeared, her hair disarranged, and her hat (**askew, crestfallen**), she certainly was a strange sight.

20. A leading (**wastrel, exponent**) of TV's importance in modern life coined the phrase "the medium is the message."

Unit 11

Definitions

Note carefully the spelling, pronunciation, and definition of each of the following words. Then write the word in the blank space in the illustrative phrase following.

1. allude
(ə 'lüd)

(*v.*) to refer to casually or indirectly

_____ to her past successes

2. clairvoyant
(klâr 'voi ənt)

(*adj.*) supernaturally perceptive; (*n.*) one who possesses extrasensory powers, seer

said to possess _____ powers

3. conclusive
(kən 'klü siv)

(*adj.*) serving to settle an issue; final

offered _____ evidence of his guilt

4. disreputable
(dis 'rep yə tə bəl)

(*adj.*) not respectable, not esteemed

unfavorably impressed by their _____ appearance

5. endemic
(en 'dem ik)

(*adj.*) native or confined to a particular region or people; characteristic of or prevalent in a field

a species _____ to the tropics

6. exemplary
(eg 'zem plə rē)

(*adj.*) worthy of imitation, commendable; serving as a model

became an _____ student

7. fathom
('fath əm)

(*v.*) to understand; get to the bottom of; determine the depth of; (*n.*) a measure of depth in water

unable to _____ his purposes

8. guile
(gīl)

(*n.*) treacherous cunning, deceit

the _____ of the legendary serpent

9. integrity
(in 'teg rə tē)

(*n.*) honesty, high moral standards, soundness; an unimpaired condition, completeness

a person of unquestionable _____

10. itinerary
(ī 'tin ə rer ē)

(*n.*) a route of travel; a record of travel; a guidebook

plan your _____ through Europe

11. misconstrue
(mis kən 'strü)

(*v.*) to interpret wrongly, mistake the meaning of

_____ his motives

12. obnoxious
(äb 'näk shəs)

(*adj.*) highly offensive, arousing strong dislike

angered by his _____ remarks

13. placate
('plā kāt)

(*v.*) to appease, soothe, pacify

tried to _____ my angry friend

14. placid
('plas id)

(*adj.*) calm, peaceful

the _____ water of the lake

15. plagiarism
('plā jə riz əm)

(*n.*) passing off or using as one's own the writings (or other materials) of another person

accuse the author of _____

16. potent
('pōt ənt)

(*adj.*) powerful; highly effective

a _____ force for good

17. pretext
('prē tekst)

(*n.*) a false reason, deceptive excuse

find some _____ for leaving

18. protrude
(prō 'trüd)

(*v.*) to stick out, thrust forth

correct the teeth that _____

19. stark
(stärk)

(*adj., adv.*) harsh, unrelieved, desolate; utterly

shocked by the _____ contrast

20. superficial
(sü pər 'fish əl)

(*adj.*) on or near the surface; concerned with or understanding only what is on the surface, shallow

a _____ anaylsis of the problem

Completing the Sentence

From the words for this unit, choose the one that best completes each of the following sentences. Write the word in the space provided.

1. On the _____ of delivering a package, he sought to gain admission into the apartment.

2. Sherlock Holmes assured Dr. Watson that it was simple deduction, not some _____ faculty, that led him to the document's hiding place.

3. Although the cut on my arm was bleeding quite heavily, it proved to be quite _____ , and only a tight bandage was required.

4. I selected him as my business partner not only because I respect his ability but also because I have unlimited confidence in his character and

_____ .

5. Phyllis was too polite to mention John's crude behavior at the party, but she certainly _____ to it when she spoke of "undesirable elements."

6. By disregarding the flood of excuses, explanations, and justifications, we were able to _____ the true reasons for her actions.

7. When we consider the _____ misery of the last years of his life, we must conclude that he paid in full for all his offenses.

8. The tapes of the conversations were regarded as _____ proof that the official had been aware of the crime.

9. If you allow your foot to _____ into the aisle, someone may trip over it.

10. His skillful use of flattery and double-talk to persuade us to agree to his scheme was a typical example of his _____ .

11. Though I was entirely innocent of the infraction of the dress code, the teacher _____ my silence as an admission of guilt.

12. We spent many pleasant hours poring over all kinds of maps and guide books, planning the _____ for our trip across the continent.

13. Too many young people, in an attempt to achieve a casual and "dashing" appearance, succeed only in looking sloppy and _____ .

14. Neither misfortunes nor happy events seem to have the slightest effect on her _____ disposition.

15. Blue jeans, once _____ to the cowboys of the American West, are now a familiar part of the whole world's wardrobe.

16. Their idea of a(n) _____ student is someone so perfect in so many ways that he or she would be too good to exist.

17. The "brilliant" essay for which he received so much lavish praise has been exposed as a skillful act of _____ .

18. America's most _____ weapon in the struggle for world influence is our great tradition of democracy and freedom.

19. It is quite useless to try to _____ "dissatisfied" customers who actually enjoy being angry and making complaints.

20. His conceit and his cold disregard of other people's feelings make him utterly _____ !

Synonyms   *From the words for this unit, choose the one that is most nearly **the same** in meaning as each of the following groups of expressions. Write the word on the line provided at the right.*

1. to misjudge, misinterpret   _____

2. honesty, rectitude, probity; soundness   _____

3. disgraceful, discreditable, shady   _____

4. undisturbed, tranquil, quiet, serene   _____

5. trickery, deceit, duplicity, cunning, chicanery   _____

6. a pretense, cover story; a rationale, evasion   _____

7. decisive, indisputable, convincing; definitive   _____

8. native, indigenous; restricted to _____

9. to grasp, comprehend, figure out, plumb _____

10. mighty, formidable; forcible _____

11. skin-deep, insubstantial; cursory, slapdash _____

12. to hint at, suggest, insinuate, intimate _____

13. sheer, downright; grim, bleak; absolutely _____

14. to satisfy, mollify, allay, conciliate _____

15. insightful, discerning, uncanny; a visionary _____

16. to project, jut out, bulge _____

17. praiseworthy, meritorious, sterling; illustrative _____

18. a route; a schedule, program _____

19. disagreeable, repugnant, hateful, odious _____

20. piracy, theft _____

Antonyms   *From the words for this unit, choose the one that is most nearly **opposite** in meaning to each of the following groups of expressions. Write the word on the line provided at the right.*

1. deep, profound; thorough, exhaustive _____

2. dishonesty, corruption, turpitude _____

3. weak, inept, feckless; powerless, ineffective _____

4. honest, aboveboard; respectable, creditable _____

5. alien, foreign, extraneous _____

6. candor, artlessness, naïveté, plain dealing _____

7. unsettled, up in the air; provisional, indefinite _____

8. to vex, irk, provoke, exasperate, annoy _____

9. bright, cheerful; embellished, ornate _____

10. stormy, agitated, turbulent, tempestuous _____

11. infamous, notorious, scandalous, disreputable _____

12. agreeable, pleasing, engaging, personable _____

13. blind, unseeing, myopic, dense, imperceptive _____

Choosing the Right Word   *Encircle the **boldface** word that more satisfactorily completes each of the following sentences.*

1. The assumption that we can continue to use our natural resources as wastefully as we have in the past is (**disreputable, stark**) madness.

2. In times of crisis, the utmost care must be taken to prevent ordinary military maneuvers from being (**placated, misconstrued**) as hostile acts.

3. Do not be taken in by any (**superficial, conclusive**) resemblances between their half-baked ideas and the sensible program we proposed.

4. For as long as human beings have been able to think they have tried to (**fathom, allude**) the mysteries of the universe.

5. I find no one more (**obnoxious, clairvoyant**) than a person who insists on talking instead of listening to the brilliant and important things I have to say.

6. Instead of (**alluding, protruding**) so often to your own achievements and successes, why not wait for other people to mention them?

7. Mother was as upset as any of us, but she managed to conceal her fears so that she looked positively (**stark, placid**).

8. Of Sybil's ability to divine another person's secrets, it is hard to say where the psychologist leaves off and the (**clairvoyant, itinerary**) begins.

9. It is all very well for science fiction writers to speculate, but is there any (**exemplary, conclusive**) evidence that UFO's exist?

10. A candidate for the highest office in the land should be, above all, a person of unshakable (**guile, integrity**).

11. Phyllis produced a convenient headache as her (**pretext, itinerary**) for having to leave early.

12. Carl maintains that intelligent life must exist elsewhere in the universe, but I firmly believe that it is (**endemic, conclusive**) to Earth.

13. Why not include Mount Vernon in the (**plagiarism, itinerary**) of our spring vacation?

14. If the British government had made a sincere effort to (**misconstrue, placate**) the colonists, would the American Revolution have occurred?

15. Is it any wonder that his parents are worried, knowing that their son is associating with such a (**placid, disreputable**) group of teenagers?

16. In that neighborhood of small homes, a few massive apartment buildings (**pretext, protrude**) like giants set down in a community of dwarfs.

17. Although most of us cannot hope to match her pure idealism, we may regard her noble life as inspiring and (**exemplary, conclusive**).

18. It was clear that her book review was so similar to a review in a newspaper that it constituted an outright (**integrity, plagiarism**).

19. Walter's brilliant record as a science major at Cal Tech seems to me a (**stark, potent**) argument for taking four full years of mathematics in high school.

20. Tom Sawyer used (**guile, pretext**) to get the other boys to do his work by convincing them that whitewashing a fence was fun.

Unit 12

Definitions

Note carefully the spelling, pronunciation, and definition of each of the following words. Then write the word in the blank space in the illustrative phrase following.

1. **abjure**
   (ab 'jür)

   (*v.*) to renounce, repudiate under oath; to avoid, shun

   solemnly _____ his mistaken beliefs

2. **acrid**
   ('ak rid)

   (*adj.*) harsh in taste or odor; sharp in manner or temper

   the _____ stench of burning rubber

3. **august**
   (ô 'gəst)

   (*adj.*) majestic, inspiring admiration and respect

   the Senator's _____ appearance

4. **callous**
   ('ka ləs)

   (*adj.*) emotionally hardened, unfeeling

   his _____ disregard of my wishes

5. **clandestine**
   (klan 'des tən)

   (*adj.*) secret, concealed; underhand

   a spy's _____ activities

6. **compunction**
   (kəm 'pəŋk shən)

   (*n.*) remorse, regret

   felt no _____ for their crimes

7. **conflagration**
   (kän flə 'grā shən)

   (*n.*) a large destructive fire

   a _____ that left the city in ruins

8. **elated**
   (i 'lā tid)

   (*adj., part.*) in high spirits, jubilant; extremely pleased

   _____ by their success

9. **indelible**
   (in 'del ə bəl)

   (*adj.*) not able to be erased or removed; memorable

   use _____ ink for the records

10. **indulgent**
    (in 'dəl jənt)

    (*adj.*) yielding to the wishes or demands of others

    spoiled by his _____ guardian

11. **inveterate**
    (in 'vet ər ət)

    (*adj.*) firmly established, long-standing; habitual

    an _____ gum chewer

12. **irrelevant**
    (i 'rel ə vənt)

    (*adj.*) not to the point, not applicable or pertinent

    eliminate all _____ details

13. **nocturnal**
    (näk 'tər nəl)

    (*adj.*) of or occurring in the night

    listen to the calls of the _____ owl

14. **platitude**
    ('plat ə tüd)

    (*n.*) a commonplace, stale, or trite remark

    bored by a speech filled with _____

15. **quell**
    (kwel)

    (*v.*) to subdue, put down forcibly

    call out the police to _____ the riot

16. **quiescent**
    (kwī 'es ənt)

    (*adj.*) inactive; at rest

    a temporarily _____ geyser

17. ruminate
('rü mə nāt)

(v.) to meditate, think about at length; to chew the cud

_____ on the events of his youth

18. tacit
('tas it)

(adj.) unspoken, silent; implied, inferred

have a _____ understanding

19. tangible
('tan jə bəl)

(adj.) capable of being touched; real, concrete

the _____ results of the plan

20. trenchant
('tren chənt)

(adj.) incisive, keen; forceful, effective; cutting, caustic; distinct, clear-cut

impressed by her _____ remarks

Completing the Sentence

From the words for this unit, choose the one that best completes each of the following sentences. Write the word in the space provided.

1. There was no _____ evidence of his sincerity, but somehow we were confident that he would do all he could to help us.

2. Your statement may be correct, but since it has no bearing on the point now under discussion, I must reject it as _____ .

3. Although the disease had been _____ for several years, the doctors warned him that its symptoms could appear again at any time.

4. Though we were angry with each other, we had a(n) _____ agreement to act politely in front of Mother.

5. The fumes released by the volcano were so _____ that they caused great discomfort among people in the nearby villages.

6. How can we possibly accept the testimony of someone who is known to be a(n) _____ liar?

7. If adequate measures are not taken to control a small fire, it may become a raging _____ .

8. The audience seemed to be stirred by the speaker's remarks, but in my opinion they were no more than a series of _____ .

9. Abraham Lincoln's plan for reconstruction simply had the former rebels _____ allegiance to the Confederacy and vow to support the Union.

10. Who wouldn't be _____ at winning that huge prize on the TV quiz show?

11. The debate was decided in our favor when Carole's _____ rebuttal tore the other side's arguments to pieces.

12. His behavior was so rude and offensive that I had no _____ about telling him to leave the house.

13. In the presence of such a(n) _____ assemblage of religious leaders, representing all the major faiths, I felt very humble.

14. She tried to _____ her feeling of panic by assuring herself that there was simply no such thing as a ghost.

15. He is so completely wrapped up in his own concerns that he often seems to be _____ to other people's feelings.

16. The streets seemed safe and familiar during the day, but now we had to face unknown _____ dangers.

17. I have no patience with a(n) _____ parent who gives in to every whim and demand of an undisciplined child.

18. I stretched out under the old maple tree in the backyard and began to _____ on the strange events of that remarkable day.

19. The years of close association with outstanding personalities had left a(n) _____ mark on the students' characters.

20. The documents showed that, years before, the companies had made a(n) _____ agreement to divide the market among them.

Synonyms   From the words for this unit, choose the one that is most nearly **the same** in meaning as each of the following groups of expressions. Write the word on the line provided at the right.

1. overjoyed, jubilant, ecstatic, "tickled pink"   _____

2. persisting, chronic, dyed-in-the-wool   _____

3. to suppress, pacify, squelch, quash, crush   _____

4. a holocaust, wildfire   _____

5. to ponder, reflect, mull over, muse   _____

6. lenient, permissive, tolerant, liberal   _____

7. stately, dignified, exalted, venerable   _____

8. covert, furtive, surreptitious, stealthy   _____

9. nighttime, under cover of darkness   _____

10. insensitive, unsympathetic, thick-skinned   _____

11. still, inert, motionless, dormant, tranquil   _____

12. lasting, permanent; unforgettable   _____

13. irritating, stinging, bitter, caustic _____

14. perceptible, actual, evident, palpable _____

15. a scruple, qualm, misgiving, contrition _____

16. penetrating, cutting, telling, acute _____

17. unexpressed, unvoiced, understood, implicit _____

18. to forswear, retract, recant; to abstain from _____

19. a cliché, truism, bromide _____

20. inapplicable, immaterial, beside the point _____

Antonyms　　From the words for this unit, choose the one that is most nearly **opposite** in meaning to each of the following groups of expressions. Write the word on the line provided at the right.

1. depressed, crestfallen, despondent, "blue" _____

2. sensitive, compassionate, tenderhearted _____

3. open, overt, undisguised, aboveboard _____

4. active, thriving, lively, bustling; volatile _____

5. pertinent, material, apropos, germane _____

6. dull, bland, insipid, vapid, imperceptive _____

7. gentle, soothing, mild _____

8. an epigram, quip, witticism, bon mot _____

9. to affirm, avow, aver, profess _____

10. erasable, impermanent, ephemeral _____

11. strict, severe, inflexible, hard-nosed _____

12. humble, base, mean, lowly, abject _____

13. immaterial, imperceptible, insubstantial _____

14. to incite, provoke, arouse, foment, stir up _____

15. explicit, express, specific _____

16. sporadic, intermittent, occasional _____

17. a deluge, flood _____

18. daytime, diurnal _____

19. shamelessness, insouciance, nonchalance _____

Choosing the Right Word *Encircle the **boldface** word that more satisfactorily completes each of the following sentences.*

1. It is true that the population of the Soviet Union was slightly larger than our own, but that fact was (**callous, irrelevant**) to the question of military strength.

2. After the Senator's (**trenchant, tacit**) analysis, each of us should have a clear idea of what is involved and where we stand on the issue.

3. Just before going to sleep, we set traps to discourage the (**indelible, nocturnal**) raids of the raccoons on our food supply.

4. In these days of Presidential primaries, candidates can no longer be chosen at (**clandestine, august**) meetings of a few powerful politicians.

5. Your (**ruminations, compunctions**) on the "meaning of life" will be just a waste of time unless they lead to some plans for rational behavior.

6. The deep-seated resentment of the populace, which had been (**quiescent, irrelevant**) for years, suddenly blossomed into open rebellion.

7. The need for careful planning of college applications has been (**indelibly, callously**) impressed on the mind of every senior.

8. George Orwell uses words to express his meaning exactly and vividly, while avoiding meaningless generalities and feeble (**indelibles, platitudes**).

9. Since mother offered no objections, I felt that we had her (**acrid, tacit**) consent to go ahead with our plans for a summer trip to California.

10. Like so many (**clandestine, inveterate**) smokers, she has found that great self-discipline is needed to break the cigarette habit.

11. Millions of Americans were thrilled as they witnessed on TV the simple but (**august, callous**) ceremonies of the Presidential inauguration.

12. Although there was no (**tangible, inveterate**) reason for my alarm, I could not shake off the feeling that something terrible was about to happen.

13. We should not seek to (**quell, elate**) the idealism and enthusiasm of youth, but rather to direct those impulses into useful channels.

14. When we asked him to contribute to the charity drive, he dismissed us with the (**acrid, indulgent**) remark, "Not interested."

15. The superpowers intervened to prevent the brushfire war from engulfing the entire region in a full-scale (**conflagration, compunction**).

16. As part of the settlement, the company must henceforth (**ruminate, abjure**) unsubstantiated claims for its product.

17. Because her misconduct was clearly deliberate, we have no feelings of (**compunction, platitude**) in sentencing her to ten days of detention.

18. Taking third place in the hundred-meter dash in the intramural track meet left me satisfied but scarcely (**callous, elated**).

19. Judge Burnham has a reputation for being (**indulgent, tacit**)—but not when confronting a teenager charged with reckless driving.

20. We may criticize Americans for many things, but they are never (**elated, callous**) when appeals for help come from distressed people.

Analogies   *In each of the following, encircle the item that best completes the comparison.*

1. **conflagration** is to **brush fire** as
a. blizzard is to avalanche
b. deluge is to monsoon
c. tornado is to drought
d. hurricane is to shower

2. **blithe** is to **glum** as
a. garrulous is to talkative
b. pertinent is to irrelevant
c. august is to clandestine
d. sinuous is to quiescent

3. **indelible** is to **erase** as
a. insuperable is to conquer
b. indulgent is to pamper
c. inveterate is to refine
d. unfathomable is to misconstrue

4. **acrid** is to **smell** as
a. disheveled is to hear
b. tacit is to see
c. callous is to taste
d. tangible is to touch

5. **quell** is to **quash** as
a. covet is to shun
b. fathom is to dive
c. acquiesce is to comply
d. protrude is to abjure

6. **miser** is to **amass** as
a. exponent is to allude
b. vanguard is to conclude
c. wastrel is to squander
d. dent is to protrude

7. **placate** is to **provoke** as
a. profess is to avow
b. profess is to disclaim
c. profess is to lament
d. profess is to allure

8. **exponent** is to **pro** as
a. advocate is to con
b. opponent is to pro
c. adversary is to con
d. critic is to pro

9. **august** is to **abject** as
a. callous is to insensitive
b. placid is to tempestuous
c. tacit is to verbatim
d. clandestine is to furtive

10. **sonorous** is to **sound** as
a. august is to season
b. aromatic is to smell
c. sinuous is to taste
d. callous is to touch

11. **guile** is to **unfavorable** as
a. integrity is to favorable
b. clairvoyance is to unfavorable
c. plagiarism is to favorable
d. itinerary is to unfavorable

12. **crestfallen** is to **down** as
a. lamentable is to up
b. blithe is to down
c. elated is to up
d. nocturnal is to down

13. **exemplary** is to **favorable** as
a. disreputable is to unfavorable
b. obnoxious is to favorable
c. august is to unfavorable
d. garrulous is to favorable

14. **cow** is to **ruminate** as
a. mammal is to mole
b. rodent is to gnaw
c. amphibian is to fly
d. reptile is to hibernate

15. **fathom** is to **depth** as
a. width is to meter
b. bushel is to height
c. knot is to speed
d. inch is to yard

16. **platitude** is to **banal** as
a. respite is to arduous
b. pretext is to contentious
c. misnomer is to erroneous
d. vanguard is to tacit

17. **clairvoyant** is to **insight** as
a. potent is to power
b. garrulous is to silence
c. callous is to sympathy
d. indulgent is to harshness

18. **impostor** is to **guile** as
a. swindler is to integrity
b. peacemaker is to contentious
c. wastrel is to thrift
d. siren is to allure

Identification *In each of the following groups, encircle the word that is best defined or suggested by the introductory phrase.*

1. put down a disturbance
a. allure   b. ruminate   c. acquiesce   d. quell

2. blessed with second sight
a. crestfallen   b. clairvoyant   c. nocturnal   d. trenchant

3. "The early bird gets the worm."
a. compunction   b. platitude   c. allure   d. respite

4. dyed-in-the-wool
a. callous   b. stark   c. disheveled   d. inveterate

5. spends like there's no tomorrow
a. integrity   b. guile   c. wastrel   d. itinerary

6. ears that stand out conspicuously
a. protrude   b. placate   c. abjure   d. allude

7. a sense of guilt or uncertainty about some action
a. compunction   b. retribution   c. vanguard   d. guile

8. the fire that destroyed Chicago in 1871
a. wastrel   b. conflagration   c. nocturnal   d. allure

9. make an indirect reference to your athletic achievements
a. plagiarize   b. acquiesce   c. misconstrue   d. allude

10. get to the bottom of the situation
a. protrude   b. fathom   c. quell   d. covet

11. an eye for an eye
a. pretext   b. clairvoyant   c. retribution   d. plagiarism

12. said of a chatterbox
a. garrulous   b. lamentable   c. alluring   d. sonorous

13. happy-go-lucky
a. blithe   b. contentious   c. sinuous   d. superficial

14. "I take it all back."
a. covet   b. ruminate   c. profess   d. abjure

15. artists experimenting in new forms and techniques
a. platitude   b. vanguard   c. itinerary   d. starkness

16. a cover story
a. plagiarism   b. pretext   c. retribution   d. irrelevancy

17. an awe-inspiring religious ceremony
a. crestfallen   b. trenchant   c. elated   d. august

18. bats and other such creatures
a. quiescent   b. nocturnal   c. crestfallen   d. sinuous

19. a time-out in a hotly contested basketball game
a. respite   b. misnomer   c. pretext   d. wastrel

20. a style that is simple, unadorned, harsh
a. placid   b. nocturnal   c. stark   d. tangible

Shades of Meaning

Read each sentence carefully. Then encircle the item that best completes the statement below the sentence.

For a time she settled down; but soon the allure of the open road proved irresistible, and she was off on her travels again. **(2)**

1. In line 1 the word **allure** most nearly means
a. vitality
b. appeal
c. wanderlust
d. rewards

To determine the value of the expression $(x + y)^3$, multiply the sum of the variables x and y by the exponent 3. **(2)**

2. The word **exponent** in line 2 is best defined as
a. power
b. interpreter
c. advocate
d. number

When I checked the printed itinerary, I was astonished to find that we had been allowed exactly one hour to "do" the British Museum. **(2)**

3. The word **itinerary** in line 1 is used to mean
a. train schedule
b. account of a trip
c. guidebook for a tour
d. route of the journey

In order to protect the integrity of the museum's collection of Scythian gold, the curator refused to part with even one small treasure—and died in Stalin's purges for his pains. **(2)**

4. In line 1 the word **integrity** is best defined as
a. uniqueness
b. completeness
c. brilliance
d. probity

Since the middle class barely existed in tsarist Russia, the division between "haves" and "have-nots" was always trenchant. **(2)**

5. The word **trenchant** in line 2 most nearly means
a. caustic
b. forceful
c. incisive
d. clear-cut

Antonyms

*In each of the following groups, encircle the word or expression that is most nearly the **opposite** of the word in **boldface type**.*

1. allure
a. discover
b. accept
c. repel
d. escape

2. contentious
a. difficult
b. twisted
c. small
d. agreeable

3. potent
a. edible
b. repeated
c. tasty
d. ineffective

4. lamentable
a. praiseworthy
b. unfortunate
c. carefree
d. honest

5. guile
a. affluence
b. frankness
c. fraud
d. sweetness

6. tacit
a. cheap
b. expressed
c. undamaged
d. talkative

7. inveterate
a. foolish
b. closed
c. ungainly
d. occasional

8. crestfallen
a. brave
b. disappointed
c. neat
d. joyful

9. **endemic**	12. **irrelevant**	15. **covet**	18. **indelible**
a. native	a. concerned	a. release	a. temporary
b. healthy	b. prompt	b. hide	b. sad
c. alien	c. appropriate	c. disdain	c. forceful
d. superficial	d. ugly	d. desire	d. certain
10. **placate**	13. **callous**	16. **quiescent**	19. **placid**
a. destroy	a. sensitive	a. deafening	a. disturbed
b. vex	b. hidden	b. inactive	b. natural
c. calm	c. tight	c. bustling	c. steep
d. enlarge	d. curved	d. certain	d. rich
11. **disreputable**	14. **conclusive**	17. **acrid**	20. **sinuous**
a. angry	a. contentious	a. sweet	a. straight
b. respected	b. final	b. sour	b. curved
c. organized	c. doubtful	c. new	c. clean
d. extreme	d. important	d. strong	d. open

Completing the Sentence

From the following list of words choose the one that best completes each of the sentences below. Write the word in the appropriate space.

Group A

allude	itinerary	lamentable	stark
misconstrue	fathom	inveterate	clandestine
respite	disreputable	garrulous	plagiarize

1. "The clearer your orders are, the less risk you run that someone will _____ them," she observed.

2. He is such a(n) _____ bridge player that he once tried to set up a game during a subway ride.

3. She wore only a single strand of pearls to set off the _____ simplicity of her black dress.

4. Although the bus driver had a rather _____ appearance, we found that he was courteous and dependable all during the journey.

5. I have an uncomfortable feeling that the hosts of late-night talk shows are _____ each other's jokes.

Group B

profess	retribution	protrude	exemplary
wastrel	placate	exponent	vanguard
tangible	pretext	contentious	elate

1. Since he has little interest in books, I suspect that his frequent trips to the library are no more than a(n) _____ to meet girls.

2. That brilliant program on urban problems has placed her firmly in the _____ of producers of TV documentaries.

3. Although he _____ to have no interest in money, I notice that he is very careful about collecting every dollar due him.

4. The police know the suspect's identity but have so far failed to uncover _____ evidence linking him to the crime.

5. When I finally understood why my sister was angry with me, I did all I could to _____ her.

Word Families

A. On the line provided, write a **noun form** of each of the following words.

EXAMPLE: tangible—**tangibility**

1. indulgent _____
2. placid _____
3. profess _____
4. protrude _____
5. lamentable _____
6. sinuous _____
7. allude _____
8. potent _____
9. conclusive _____
10. clairvoyant _____
11. ruminate _____
12. contentious _____
13. sonorous _____
14. exemplary _____
15. superficial _____
16. elated _____
17. irrelevant _____
18. quiescent _____

B. On the line provided, write a **verb** related to each of the following words.

EXAMPLE: conclusive—**conclude**

1. wastrel _____
2. indulgent _____
3. contentious _____
4. plagiarism _____
5. lamentable _____

R

Filling the Blanks

Encircle the pair of words that best complete each of the following passages.

1. Utterly _____ at their upset defeat, the Belleville squad looked on dismally as the trophy they had so much _____ was awarded to their archrivals from Henderson.
   a. lamentable . . . abjured
   b. crestfallen . . . coveted
   c. disheveled . . . ruminated
   d. blithe . . . professed

2. High winds fanned the flames, and in no time at all the _____ had spread to a nearby tire factory. Clouds of thick black smoke billowed up into the sky, and the _____ stench of burning rubber filled the air.
   a. contention . . . obnoxious
   b. retribution . . . indelible
   c. compunction . . . potent
   d. conflagration . . . acrid

3. After romping around with my six-year-old nephew all afternoon, I had become woefully _____ . My trousers were rumpled, my shirttails were hanging out, and my tie was all _____ .
   a. disheveled . . . askew
   b. disreputable . . . crestfallen
   c. garrulous . . . acrid
   d. lamentable . . . sinuous

4. I had hoped that the candidates would make a few _____ observations during the course of the debate. All I got, however, were the same tired old _____ that politicians have been mouthing for decades.
   a. irrelevant . . . plagiarisms
   b. exemplary . . . pretexts
   c. trenchant . . . platitudes
   d. superficial . . . ruminations

5. During the evening, Ned must have _____ to his close acquaintance with at least a dozen celebrities. Afterward, we all agreed that his nickname, "Name-dropper Ned," was no _____ .
   a. protruded . . . plagiarism
   b. alluded . . . misnomer
   c. misconstrued . . . pretext
   d. protruded . . . platitude

6. The trail nicknamed "Dead Man's Curves" is so steep and _____ that even the most proficient and experienced skiers often must stop for a brief _____ before completing the course.
   a. sinuous . . . respite
   b. disreputable . . . pretext
   c. stark . . . itinerary
   d. clandestine . . . compunction

7. In view of the countless crimes the dictator had committed while in power, the revolutionary tribunal expressed no _____ in seeking the sternest _____ on behalf of the people.
   a. guile . . . conflagration
   b. integrity . . . respite
   c. compunction . . . retribution
   d. pretext . . . vanguard

Cumulative Review   Units 1–12

Analogies   *In each of the following, encircle the item that best completes the comparison.*

1. insuperable is to **overcome** as
a. infallible is to explain
b. omnivorous is to eat
c. indomitable is to tame
d. feasible is to do

2. alienate is to **estrange** as
a. quell is to suppress
b. covet is to abhor
c. brandish is to waive
d. profess is to abjure

3. hair is to **unkempt** as
a. room is to musty
b. odor is to pungent
c. trunk is to commodious
d. clothing is to disheveled

4. crestfallen is to **exult** as
a. slow is to plod
b. elated is to lament
c. brash is to revel
d. apprehensive is to tremble

5. indelible is to **expunge** as
a. omniscient is to know
b. impervious is to pierce
c. omnipotent is to rule
d. invulnerable is to cure

6. explicit is to **tacit** as
a. spontaneous is to premeditated
b. suave is to urbane
c. tepid is to acrid
d. poignant is to ingenuous

7. tangible is to **touch** as
a. lamentable is to rejoice
b. amicable is to hinder
c. pliable is to bend
d. feasible is to avoid

8. trenchant is to **cut** as
a. ardent is to flow
b. sinuous is to scar
c. garrulous is to silence
d. corrosive is to burn

9. quiescent is to **repose** as
a. askew is to activity
b. turbulent is to motion
c. scrupulous is to speed
d. negligible is to significance

10. holocaust is to **conflagration** as
a. deluge is to inundation
b. famine is to plague
c. chaos is to revolution
d. earthquake is to avalanche

11. integrity is to **duplicity** as
a. clemency is to mercy
b. animosity is to rancor
c. chivalry is to gallantry
d. candor is to guile

12. disreputable is to **esteem** as
a. exemplary is to extol
b. reprehensible is to commend
c. unjust is to redress
d. ludicrous is to deride

13. covet is to **craving** as
a. abhor is to aversion
b. scrutinize is to apathy
c. esteem is to animosity
d. discern is to antagonism

14. callous is to **sensitivity** as
a. facile is to skill
b. clairvoyant is to discernment
c. stolid is to emotion
d. belligerent is to hostility

15. placid is to **tranquillity** as
a. fainthearted is to fortitude
b. diffident is to audacity
c. nonchalant is to concern
d. limpid is to clarity

16. tentative is to **conclusive** as
a. dour is to obnoxious
b. august is to destitute
c. cursory is to meticulous
d. stark is to austere

17. decor is to **opulent** as
a. sound is to sonorous
b. duty is to officious
c. discrepancy is to irrelevant
d. habit is to inveterate

18. truculent is to **contentious** as
a. craven is to intrepid
b. adroit is to deft
c. clandestine is to nocturnal
d. malevolent is to benevolent

19. potent is to **clout** as
a. voluminous is to brevity
b. tepid is to heat
c. squalid is to allure
d. cogent is to force

20. field is to **fallow** as
a. weather is to inclement
b. root is to gnarled
c. building is to decrepit
d. volcano is to dormant

21. backbone is to **fortitude** as
a. stomach is to altruism
b. cheek is to temerity
c. lip is to diffidence
d. spine is to adversity

22. hands are to **ambidextrous** as
a. adversaries are to amicable
b. moods are to ironic
c. languages are to bilingual
d. duties are to insidious

Shades of Meaning

Read each sentence carefully. Then encircle the item that best completes the statement below the sentence.

On a very cold day it takes a little ingenuity to persuade my car's recalcitrant engine to turn over. **(2)**

1. In line 2 the word **recalcitrant** most nearly means
a. lazy   b. unruly   c. resistant   d. ancient

The blithe ignorance of Marie Antoinette's famous remark, "Let them eat cake," reveals both a cold heart and a shallow education. **(2)**

2. The item that best indicates the meaning of **blithe** in line 1 is
a. witty   b. unconcerned   c. spiteful   d. genial

During his reign Henry VII made a determined effort to recover royal lands illegally alienated from the crown. **(2)**

3. The word **alienated** in line 2 most nearly means
a. stolen   b. seized   c. bought   d. transferred

          "I'll break my staff,
Bury it certain fathoms in the earth, **(2)**
And deeper than did ever plummet sound
I'll drown my book." (Shakespeare, *The Tempest,* V, 1, 61–64) **(4)**

4. In line 2 the word **fathoms** is used to mean
a. sounding lines   c. rates of speed
b. measures of depth   d. quantities of water

At first I was appalled by the self-serving hype endemic to the film industry, but a few years in Tinsel Town made it seem quite normal. **(2)**

5. The phrase **endemic to** in line 1 is best defined as
a. prevalent in   c. confined to
b. uncharacteristic of   d. resulting from

As the adults ruminated placidly in the meadow, the kids and lambs frolicked playfully among the hedgerows. **(2)**

6. The word **ruminated** in line 1 most nearly means
a. meditated   c. chewed the cud
b. locked horns   d. rested

Filling the Blanks

Encircle the pair of words that best complete the meaning of each of the following sentences.

1. Though the _____ of our summer tour does include a brief _____ in Paris, where we will stay at the world's most luxurious hotel, we will spend most of the trip exploring various points of interest in the south of France.
   a. vanguard . . . demise
   b. itinerary . . . sojourn
   c. quandary . . . respite
   d. indemnity . . . dearth

2. At first glance the painting bears a(n) _____ resemblance to something by Rembrandt, but on closer inspection the eye begins to _____ subtle differences in style and technique that show it to be the work of another painter.
   a. insidious . . . ascertain
   b. unfeigned . . . amend
   c. superficial . . . discern
   d. ominous . . . fathom

3. Though he _____ to be learned and refined, his ideas and attitudes show his mind to be woefully _____ and uncouth.
   a. professes . . . sophomoric
   b. assents . . . urbane
   c. abhors . . . suave
   d. alludes . . . supercilious

4. When the noise of his uncle's drunken _____ interrupts the quiet of the night, Prince Hamlet remarks that such _____ carousing is, to his mind, "a custom more honored in the breach than in the observance."
   a. nostalgia . . . culinary
   b. indulgence . . . clandestine
   c. solace . . . vociferous
   d. revelry . . . nocturnal

5. Though the vision of "striking it rich overnight" held such an irresistible _____ for poor Americans in 1849, most of those who were attracted to the goldfields of California ended up as _____ as they had started out.
   a. guise . . . parsimonious
   b. impetus . . . blithe
   c. allure . . . destitute
   d. pretext . . . bereft

6. I had always admired the ease and _____ with which he turned out essays and articles so effortlessly until one day I discovered that he had actually _____ three-quarters of what he claimed to be his own work.
   a. duplicity . . . retrogressed
   b. facility . . . plagiarized
   c. temerity . . . alienated
   d. diffidence . . . adulterated

Unit 13

Definitions

Note carefully the spelling, pronunciation, and definition of each of the following words. Then write the word in the blank space in the illustrative phrase following.

1. antipathy
(an 'tip ə thē)

(*n.*) a strong dislike, hostile feeling

has an _____ for spinach

2. applicable
('ap lə kə bəl)

(*adj.*) capable of being applied; relevant, suitable

not _____ to this case

3. asset
('as et)

(*n.*) something of value; a resource; an advantage

the company's _____

4. beset
(bē 'set)

(*v.*) to attack from all sides; to surround, hem in; (*part.*) harassed, troubled; studded (as with jewels)

_____ with many fears

5. compassion
(kəm 'pash ən)

(*n.*) sympathy for another's suffering; pity

felt _____ for the poor

6. decorum
(di 'kôr əm)

(*n.*) proper behavior, good taste; orderliness

disturb the _____ of the meeting

7. duress
(dù 'res)

(*n.*) compulsion by threat; forcible confinement

confessed under _____

8. exuberant
(eg 'zü bər ənt)

(*adj.*) high-spirited, enthusiastic, unrestrained; excessive, abundant

unable to control their _____ spirits

9. facsimile
(fak 'sim ə lē)

(*n.*) an exact copy

obtain a _____ of the Constitution

10. imbibe
(im 'bīb)

(*v.*) to drink; to take in, absorb

_____ knowledge from many sources

11. implacable
(im 'plak ə bəl)

(*adj.*) not to be satisfied or pacified; unyielding

fighting against an _____ enemy

12. infinitesimal
(in fin ə 'tes ə məl)

(*adj.*) so small as to be almost immeasurable; minute

an _____ amount of dust

13. innocuous
(i 'näk yü əs)

(*adj.*) harmless, inoffensive; insignificant

makes _____ remarks

14. militate
('mil ə tāt)

(*v.*) to have effect or force on or against someone or something

since the present situation _____ against the success of the undertaking

15. patent
('pat ənt)

(*n.*) exclusive rights over an invention; copyright; (*v.*) to arrange or obtain such rights; (*adj.*) plain, open to view; copyrighted

make a _____ error

16. prowess
('praù əs)

(*n.*) distinguished bravery; superior skill or ability

won fame for his military _____

17. sedate
(sə 'dāt)

(*adj.*) quiet, settled, sober; (*v.*) to administer a tranquilizer

conduct herself in a _____ manner

18. stentorian
(sten 'tôr ē ən)

(*adj.*) extremely loud

the speaker's _____ delivery

19. stipulate
('stip yə lāt)

(*v.*) to arrange specifically; to require as a condition of agreement

_____ the terms of employment

20. ultimatum
(əl tə 'mā təm)

(*n.*) a final proposal or statement of conditions

present an _____ to the enemy

Completing the Sentence

From the words for this unit, choose the one that best completes each of the following sentences. Write the word in the space provided.

1. The player's chronic shoulder injury _____ against the idea of extending his baseball career for another season.

2. The landlord's _____ was simple and direct: Pay the rent increase or get out.

3. I am well on the road to becoming a millionaire because I have just been awarded the _____ for an automatic homework machine.

4. How can you expect her to concern herself with your problems when she is so _____ with troubles of her own!

5. I must admit that I feel a strong _____ toward anyone whose table manners are as bad as Sid's.

6. I was amazed to see how a few years had transformed an unruly tomboy into a well-bred, _____ young lady.

7. Dr. Albert Schweitzer had not only great scientific ability but a deep sense of _____ for suffering humanity.

8. American law forbids a suspect to be arrested and held in any form of _____ without being formally charged.

9. He has his shortcomings, but as compared with his great services to his community and nation, they seem all but _____ .

10. His chief _____ both in business and in social life are his excellent appearance and pleasant manner.

11. The artist's latest work acclaimed by the critics seemed to me to be no more than a(n) _____ of a cardboard cereal box.

12. If only he could match his _____ on the basketball court with a high level of excellence in the classroom!

13. During the long summer afternoons, we used to sit on the shaded veranda, _____ iced drinks and talking about life.

14. The reference material you have given me is interesting, but most of it is not _____ to my term paper.

15. If the contract was framed by a good lawyer, it will _____ exactly when, where, and how payment is to be made.

16. His refusal to discuss even the possibility of a compromise convinced me that I was faced with a(n) _____ opponent.

17. We could hear the quarterback's _____ signals even above the roar of the crowd.

18. The "monster" that frightened you so much during the hike last week was just a(n) _____ water snake.

19. How quickly their _____ holiday mood became quiet and sober when they had to return to work on Monday morning!

20. I enjoy Don's jokes, but he ought to bear in mind that there are certain standards of _____ to be observed at graduation.

Synonyms   *From the words for this unit, choose the one that is most nearly **the same** in meaning as each of the following groups of expressions. Write the word on the line provided at the right.*

1. a replica, duplicate, reproduction, clone   _____

2. feeble, impotent; unobjectionable; insipid   _____

3. final terms   _____

4. seemliness, good form, propriety   _____

5. relentless, inexorable, unappeasable   _____

6. an exclusive license; evident, plain   _____

7. hostility, enmity, aversion, bad blood   _____

8. compulsion, intimidation, coercion   _____

9. a property, possession, holding, endowment   _____

10. thundering, booming, deafening, earsplitting ⎯⎯⎯⎯⎯⎯

11. unruffled, composed, cool and collected ⎯⎯⎯⎯⎯⎯

12. lively, ebullient, irrepressible; lavish ⎯⎯⎯⎯⎯⎯

13. valor, courage, heroism; mastery, proficiency ⎯⎯⎯⎯⎯⎯

14. to specify, require, contract, provide for ⎯⎯⎯⎯⎯⎯

15. to counter, oppose, work against ⎯⎯⎯⎯⎯⎯

16. tiny, minuscule, microscopic; unnoticeable ⎯⎯⎯⎯⎯⎯

17. to swallow, gulp, quaff; to assimilate, digest ⎯⎯⎯⎯⎯⎯

18. concern, pity, commiseration, empathy ⎯⎯⎯⎯⎯⎯

19. appropriate, relevant, fit, apt, apposite ⎯⎯⎯⎯⎯⎯

20. to assail, harass, badger, pester, torment ⎯⎯⎯⎯⎯⎯

Antonyms *From the words for this unit, choose the one that is most nearly **opposite** in meaning to each of the following groups of expressions. Write the word on the line provided at the right.*

1. inappropriate, unsuitable, irrelevant ⎯⎯⎯⎯⎯⎯

2. depressed, despondent, sulky ⎯⎯⎯⎯⎯⎯

3. hushed, inaudible, whispered, mute ⎯⎯⎯⎯⎯⎯

4. to eject, emit, expel, discharge ⎯⎯⎯⎯⎯⎯

5. harmful, dangerous, pernicious, toxic, virulent ⎯⎯⎯⎯⎯⎯

6. indifference, callousness, heartlessness ⎯⎯⎯⎯⎯⎯

7. vast, immense, huge, infinite ⎯⎯⎯⎯⎯⎯

8. a drawback, handicap, liability ⎯⎯⎯⎯⎯⎯

9. lenient, indulgent, permissive; flexible ⎯⎯⎯⎯⎯⎯

10. cowardice; incompetence, ineptitude ⎯⎯⎯⎯⎯⎯

11. impropriety, bad form, bad taste ⎯⎯⎯⎯⎯⎯

12. concealed, hidden, secret, clandestine ⎯⎯⎯⎯⎯⎯

13. attraction, appeal, allure, sympathy ⎯⎯⎯⎯⎯⎯

14. loud, brash; flashy, flamboyant; flighty, giddy ⎯⎯⎯⎯⎯⎯

15. persuasion, coaxing, sweet talk, cajolery ⎯⎯⎯⎯⎯⎯

16. a variation, modification, permutation ⎯⎯⎯⎯⎯⎯

Choosing the Right Word   *Encircle the **boldface** word that more satisfactorily completes each of the following sentences.*

1. We soon learned that behind the woman's modest and (**stentorian, sedate**) appearance, there were an iron determination and a sharp temper.

2. As he watched his house go up in flames, he felt that he was the victim of an (**innocuous, implacable**) fate.

3. Many of the lessons that we learned during the Great Depression are (**implacable, applicable**) to our economic problems today.

4. The politician's poor showing in the polls and the failure of his fund-raising efforts (**militated, stipulated**) against his entering the Senate race.

5. "Here's the (**ultimatum, antipathy**)," said Father: "Pass all your courses, or forget about attending the Senior Prom."

6. The mistake in identification was so (**patent, infinitesimal**) that the suspect was released with the apologies of the arresting officer.

7. Mistaking the (**sedate, stentorian**) backfire of the truck for a sudden burst of gunfire, we ducked behind a parked car for safety.

8. Although he was (**beset, stipulated**) by creditors, a tough employer, and medical problems, he never seemed to lose his zest for living.

9. You are in deep trouble if you combine a strong taste for high living with an equally strong (**antipathy, compassion**) for hard work.

10. They were so (**exuberant, innocuous**) in their praise that I soon began to suspect either their judgment or their sincerity.

11. What good does it do to include all those (**stipulations, facsimiles**) in the agreement if there are no provisions for enforcing them?

12. My study of astronomy gave me a sense of the (**infinitesimal, exuberant**) importance of man and his tiny planet in a boundless universe.

13. Jim's most valuable (**prowess, asset**) may be his ability to listen quietly, even when he doesn't fully understand what is being said.

14. It does little good to feel (**decorum, compassion**) for those less fortunate than ourselves if we are not willing to make sacrifices to help them.

15. His (**prowess, duress**) as a speaker and debater quickly made him one of the leading figures in the Senate.

16. Her sense of (**compassion, decorum**) is so strict that she often makes other people feel stiff and uncomfortable.

17. In this synthetic world of ours, I sometimes wonder if my life is genuine or just a(n) (**ultimatum, facsimile**) of the real thing.

18. The authorities suspected that the hostage's statement was not made voluntarily, but under (**duress, patent**).

19. The tough leadership we need in these troubled times will not come from uncertain and (**applicable, innocuous**) personalities.

20. Without actually understanding much of what the speaker was saying, the audience seemed to (**imbibe, beset**) her optimism and vigor.

Unit 14

| **Definitions** | Note carefully the spelling, pronunciation, and definition of each of the following words. Then write the word in the blank space in the illustrative phrase following. |

1. alacrity
(ə 'lak rə tē)

(n.) a cheerful readiness; brisk and eager action

respond with _____

2. alleviate
(ə 'lē vē āt)

(v.) to relieve, make more bearable

_____ the patient's pain

3. antithesis
(an 'tith ə sis)

(n.) the direct opposite; a sharp contrast

the _____ of what I had hoped for

4. appall
(ə 'pôl)

(v.) to fill with dismay or horror

_____ at the thought of another war

5. bellicose
('bel i kōs)

(adj.) warlike in manner or temperament; quarrelsome

_____ young army officers

6. disparage
(dis 'pâr ij)

(v.) to belittle, speak slightingly of; to undervalue

resented his efforts to _____ us

7. dissonant
('dis ə nənt)

(adj.) not in harmony; disagreeing, at odds

the piercing clamor of _____ voices

8. droll
(drōl)

(adj.) amusingly odd

delighted by her _____ wit

9. edict
('ē dikt)

(n.) an order issued by someone in authority

ruled by royal _____

10. elucidate
(i 'lü sə dāt)

(v.) to clarify, explain

try to _____ the text

11. laud
(lôd)

(v.) to praise

_____ the students for their grades

12. loll
(läl)

(v.) to act in a lazy manner, lounge; to recline, droop

_____ in the hammock

13. loquacious
(lō 'kwā shəs)

(adj.) talkative, wordy; fond of talking

impatient with the _____ chairman

14. magnanimous
(mag 'nan ə məs)

(adj.) generous in forgiving, above small meannesses

_____ toward his former enemies

15. mandatory
('man də tôr ē)

(adj.) required, obligatory

receive a _____ increase in salary

16. nondescript
('nän də skript)

(adj.) ordinary, not outstanding; not easily classified

not pleased with the _____ clothing

17. phlegmatic
(fleg 'mat ik)

(*adj.*) slow-moving, sluggish; unemotional

impatient with his _____ disposition

18. rescind
(ri 'sind)

(*v.*) to repeal, cancel

_____ earlier laws

19. vivacious
(və 'vā shəs)

(*adj.*) lively, sprightly, full of energy

enjoy the company of _____ youths

20. whet
(whet)

(*v.*) to sharpen, make keen or eager

served to _____ my curiosity

Completing the Sentence

From the words for this unit, choose the one that best completes each of the following sentences. Write the word in the space provided.

1. The principal finally _____ the unfair school regulation that prevented new students from trying out for the varsity teams.

2. I much preferred to enjoy the paintings quietly, without listening to the "explanations" of the _____ guide.

3. Even the state troopers, who had been hardened by long experience, were _____ when they came on the scene of the automobile accident.

4. George's disposition is so _____ that he is apt to turn a simple difference of opinion into a full-scale donnybrook.

5. I shall never forget Lucy's _____ offer to coach me, even though we were competing for the same role in the play.

6. In spite of her inexperience as a programmer, she attacked her new job with _____ and made good progress.

7. At that dull, stodgy party, her _____ personality was like a breath of fresh air.

8. You can make requests and suggestions if you wish, but please don't issue any _____ .

9. Instead of waiting for government help, let's do all we can right now to _____ the sufferings of the flood victims.

10. His enthusiastic and colorful description of the new series on public TV has _____ my desire to see it.

11. Unlike Stan, I have never been in France, but is that any reason for him to _____ my efforts to speak French?

12. Although in America voting is not _____ , every qualified citizen has a duty to go to the polls in every election.

13. His idle, pleasure-seeking way of life is the exact _____ of all that his hardworking parents had expected of him.

14. Though her friends _____ her achievements, her enemies ridiculed them.

15. When the speaker tried to _____ his explanation of solar energy, I became more confused than ever.

16. I'm usually quite energetic, but there are times when I want to do nothing but _____ about and listen to my favorite albums.

17. Is this _____ little house the "magnificent mansion" that you've been telling us about all these weeks?

18. Maggie's sarcastic remarks introduced a(n) _____ note into what had been a harmonious meeting.

19. He may appear to be _____ , but his friends are aware of the strong emotions simmering beneath his quiet exterior.

20. In a time of fast-talking, slambang comedians, is there a place for his kind of quiet, _____ humor?

21. Eager to get to the beach early, we accepted Rae's offer of a ride with _____ .

22. If you hope to get a teaching license someday, you will have to meet all the _____ requirements.

23. What a difference between the nervous, high-strung thoroughbred and the _____ packhorse!

Synonyms   *From the words for this unit, choose the one that is most nearly **the same** in meaning as each of the following groups of expressions. Write the word on the line provided at the right.*

1. unselfish, charitable, noble, bighearted   _____

2. grating, strident, unmelodious; irreconcilable   _____

3. to hail, extol, glorify, exalt   _____

4. to interpret, expound, explicate   _____

5. lively, spirited, animated, ebullient   _____

6. to hone, put an edge on; to excite, stimulate   _____

7. gossipy, voluble, garrulous; long-winded   _____

8. comical, humorous, whimsical, zany   _____

9. to withdraw, revoke, retract, annul, abrogate   _____

10. the opposite, contrary, antipode _____

11. lethargic, indolent, torpid; stolid, impassive _____

12. promptness, willingness, dispatch, celerity _____

13. plain, unremarkable, ordinary, unimpressive _____

14. compulsory, requisite; imperative _____

15. aggressive, combative, belligerent _____

16. to shock, stun, stupefy; horrify _____

17. a command, decree, proclamation _____

18. to degrade, decry, run down; to underrate _____

19. to lessen, lighten, allay, mitigate, assuage _____

20. to lounge, loaf, loiter; to sag, dangle _____

Antonyms *From the words for this unit, choose the one that is most nearly **opposite** in meaning to each of the following groups of expressions. Write the word on the line provided at the right.*

1. to obscure, becloud, muddy up, obfuscate _____

2. petty, selfish; unforgiving, spiteful _____

3. to criticize, censure, belittle, disparage _____

4. humorless, solemn, dour _____

5. harmonious, agreeing, euphonious _____

6. emotional, sensitive, thin-skinned; excitable _____

7. distinctive, remarkable, vivid, prepossessing _____

8. optional, voluntary, discretionary _____

9. silent, reticent, closemouthed, terse, taciturn _____

10. to praise, extol, laud; to "plug" _____

11. amicable, peaceable, conciliatory, pacific _____

12. dull, spiritless, listless, indolent, languid _____

13. to dull, blunt; to deaden, stifle, dampen _____

14. to please, cheer, gladden, elate, exhilarate _____

15. reluctance, unwillingness, hesitancy _____

16. to affirm, endorse, uphold, ratify _____

Choosing the Right Word   *Encircle the **boldface** word that more satisfactorily completes each of the following sentences.*

1. In the fight against air pollution, many states have made filtering devices (**phlegmatic, mandatory**) for all cars sold within their borders.

2. The cake was delicious, but the serving was so small that it did little more than (**elucidate, whet**) my appetite.

3. The only truly effective way to (**alleviate, appall**) the poverty of third-world nations is to help increase their capacity to produce wealth.

4. I see no reason to (**laud, elucidate**) him in such glowing terms for doing no more than his duty.

5. Her manner of speaking is so (**phlegmatic, vivacious**) that even her most commonplace remarks seem to suggest charm and excitement.

6. Observers doubted that any coalition composed of such (**magnanimous, dissonant**) factions could long refrain from petty infighting.

7. Edna pretended to be indifferent about going to the dance, but I noticed that she accepted Harry's invitation with (**loquacity, alacrity**).

8. I am waiting for you to (**elucidate, alleviate**) those ambiguous remarks about my family tree!

9. Because of the incidents that occurred during hazing week, the school may (**whet, rescind**) the rules that allow fraternity initiations.

10. In the eyes of such leaders as Gandhi and Martin Luther King, violence is the very (**edict, antithesis**) of a civilized society.

11. There is an old tradition that women are more (**loquacious, phlegmatic**) than men, but all the men I know do their full share of talking.

12. His jokes were actually not too good, but his (**nondescript, droll**) manner of delivering them made a big hit with the audience.

13. There must be a serious flaw in the character of those who make it a habit to (**alleviate, disparage**) the abilities of their best friends.

14. The houses in that development are a mixture of (**vivacious, nondescript**) styles, with no particular architectural character or taste.

15. Churchill told his countrymen to be resolute in war, defiant in defeat, and (**magnanimous, loquacious**) in victory.

16. What (**appalled, alleviated**) us even more than the fearful living conditions was the fact that the refugees seemed to have lost all hope.

17. Only an unusually (**phlegmatic, vivacious**) person could have remained calm in the face of such provocation.

18. The expression "What goes up must come down" might be termed an (**antithesis, edict**) of nature.

19. Would you rather (**droll, loll**) in the back seat of a chauffeured limousine, or drive your own convertible?

20. Although Americans are not a (**bellicose, phlegmatic**) people, they have proven themselves prepared to defend their nation at any cost.

Unit 15

Definitions

Note carefully the spelling, pronunciation, and definition of each of the following words. Then write the word in the blank space in the illustrative phrase following.

1. **abrasive**
   (ə 'brā siv)

   (*adj.*) causing irritation, harsh; grinding or wearing down; (*n.*) a substance used to smooth or polish

   angered by your _____ words

2. **acclimate**
   ('ak lə māt)

   (*v.*) to adapt to a new climate, environment, or situation

   _____ oneself to a new school

3. **chagrin**
   (shə 'grin)

   (*n.*) irritation or humiliation caused by disappointment or frustration; (*v.*) to cause such a feeling

   feel _____ at not being invited

4. **complacent**
   (kəm 'plā sənt)

   (*adj.*) self-satisfied; overly content

   a _____ air of superiority

5. **concur**
   (kən 'kər)

   (*v.*) to express agreement, approve

   _____ with the decision of the group

6. **defamation**
   (def ə 'mā shən)

   (*n.*) slander or libel

   sue for _____ of character

7. **explicate**
   ('eks plə kāt)

   (*v.*) to make plain or clear, explain; to interpret

   _____ a theorem in geometry

8. **fracas**
   ('frā kəs)

   (*n.*) a noisy quarrel or brawl

   involved in a violent street _____

9. **grotesque**
   (grō 'tesk)

   (*adj.*) unnatural, distorted; bizarre

   the gargoyle's _____ face

10. **pandemonium**
    (pan də 'mō nē əm)

    (*n.*) a wild uproar, din, or commotion

    fell into a state of _____

11. **raucous**
    ('rô kəs)

    (*adj.*) disagreeably harsh-sounding; disorderly

    _____ yelling at the wrestling match

12. **receptive**
    (ri 'sep tiv)

    (*adj.*) open and responsive to ideas or suggestions

    not _____ to criticism of their work

13. **renounce**
    (ri 'naůns)

    (*v.*) to give up or resign something

    _____ her share of the reward

14. **repress**
    (ri 'pres)

    (*v.*) to hold back; to put down or check by force

    _____ an impulse to cough

15. **reticent**
    ('ret ə sənt)

    (*adj.*) not inclined to speak; reserved; reluctant

    _____ about expressing her opinions

16. savory
('sāv ə rē)

(*adj.*) tasty; appetizing; pungent or salty, not sweet; inoffensive, respectable

the _____ odor of pizza

17. somnolent
('säm nə lənt)

(*adj.*) sleepy, drowsy; inducing sleep

arouse the _____ students

18. vehement
('vē ə mənt)

(*adj.*) intense, forceful, powerful

_____ objections to the plan

19. voluble
('väl yə bəl)

(*adj.*) characterized by a ready flow of words; glib, fluent

a _____ door-to-door salesperson

20. zealous
('zel əs)

(*adj.*) eager, earnest, devoted

a _____ follower of the Indian guru

Completing the Sentence

From the words for this unit, choose the one that best completes each of the following sentences. Write the word in the space provided.

1. I was confident that after Dad had eaten a good meal, he would be in a

   more _____ mood to my request for the use of the car.

2. When he first went out for the team, he was just an average player, but we

   all admired his _____ efforts to improve his game.

3. Although I am afraid of the dentist, I must _____ my fears and go for treatment.

4. _____ shouts and boos from the stands will have no effect on a good umpire's decisions.

5. The carpenter used a(n)_____ to remove the old finish from the top of the desk before revarnishing it.

6. The library became a scene of _____ when those "practical jokers" released a number of mice.

7. I have great respect for your knowledge of our government, but I cannot

   _____ with your opinion about the role of the judiciary.

8. There I was at the chalkboard unable to solve the problem while the entire

   class looked on. What _____ !

9. The answers the candidate gave at the press conference were rambling

   and _____ but contained practically no hard information.

10. Since hockey players often crash into each other at high speed, it's not

    surprising that occasionally a(n) _____ develops.

11. He tried hard to remain awake after dinner, but the _____ atmosphere of the musty old parlor was too much for him.

12. When we reached Mexico City, at an elevation of over 7000 feet, we found it difficult at first to _____ ourselves to the thinner air.

13. The editorial on city government was so unfair and biased that it amounted to _____ of all the elected officials of this community.

14. In an amazingly short time and with only the simplest ingredients, Bob had a(n) _____ stew simmering on the stove.

15. An accountant tried to _____ the new tax legislation to me, but when she had finished, I felt even further in the dark than before.

16. We didn't expect such _____ dislike of country-and-western music from a native of Nashville.

17. A free people cannot afford to grow _____ but must remain ever vigilant in safeguarding their liberties.

18. For Halloween the children made _____ masks that they were sure would terrorize the neighbors.

19. Both sons agreed to _____ claims to their father's estate in favor of their widowed mother.

20. The conceited actor was anything but _____ in discussing his innumerable triumphs on the stage, screen, and TV.

Synonyms   *From the words for this unit, choose the one that is most nearly **the same** in meaning as each of the following groups of expressions. Write the word on the line provided at the right.*

1. to repudiate, disown; to abdicate, abjure   _____

2. to clarify, elucidate, untangle, spell out   _____

3. boisterous, clamorous, disorderly, strident   _____

4. smug, self-satisfied, pleased with oneself   _____

5. chaos, tumult, bedlam, a three-ring circus   _____

6. groggy, nodding off; soporific   _____

7. vexation, mortification; to abash, mortify   _____

8. loquacious, garrulous; long-winded, prolix   _____

9. a row, altercation, rhubarb, brouhaha   _____

10. to subdue, curb, stifle, to constrain, bottle up   _____

11. emphatic, fierce, vigorous, impassioned   _____

12. vilification, calumny, mudslinging   _____

13. open-minded, tolerant; amenable _____

14. delectable, flavorful, aromatic, piquant _____

15. ardent, fervent, devout, dogged, "gung ho" _____

16. to grow accustomed, learn the ropes _____

17. to agree, assent; to ratify, sanction _____

18. taciturn, closemouthed, tight-lipped _____

19. fantastic, outlandish; ugly, deformed _____

20. chafing, grating, rasping, erosive _____

Antonyms From the words for this unit, choose the one that is most nearly **opposite** in meaning to each of the following groups of expressions. Write the word on the line provided at the right.

1. to confuse, bewilder; to obscure, obfuscate _____

2. placid, tranquil, peaceful, serene, pastoral _____

3. to retain, secure; to affirm, assent, aver _____

4. discontented, chagrined _____

5. distasteful, unpalatable; malodorous _____

6. talkative, garrulous, voluble, long-winded _____

7. alert, lively, wide-awake; stimulating _____

8. a salute, tribute, testimonial; praise _____

9. narrow-minded, intolerant, hidebound _____

10. smooth, polished, satiny; oily, unctuous _____

11. to differ, disagree, part company _____

12. uncommunicative, reticent, taciturn; terse _____

13. jubilation, exultation, triumph; to exult, delight _____

14. appealing, attractive, comely _____

15. order, calm, tranquility, peace, repose _____

16. to liberate, set loose; to provoke, excite _____

17. reluctant, unwilling, averse, hanging back _____

18. agreement, accord, unanimity, harmony _____

19. apathetic, lukewarm; subdued, muted _____

Choosing the Right Word   *Encircle the **boldface** word that more satisfactorily completes each of the following sentences.*

1. We all have impulses to violence, but if we are to live in a civilized society, we must learn to (**repress, concur**) them.

2. After a month in the country, we found the sounds of rush-hour traffic in the big city more (**raucous, receptive**) than ever.

3. He has a good deal of ability, but his (**zealous, abrasive**) personality has prevented him from getting ahead in the business world.

4. (**Pandemonium, Defamation**) erupted when the nervous theater manager announced to the waiting crowd that the rock concert was cancelled.

5. It's not surprising that after so many years in the Marine Corps, he has found it difficult to become (**acclimated, repressed**) to civilian life.

6. A (**fracas, defamation**) between rival groups on the floor of the convention was swiftly quelled by security men.

7. He was, I am afraid, more (**zealous, voluble**) in promoting his own career than in seeking to help the people who had elected him.

8. Mr. Sanderson is usually a man of very few words, but he was certainly (**abrasive, voluble**) when we asked him about his operation.

9. Gloria's kind words put me in such a (**receptive, savory**) frame of mind that I agreed to work on the committee before I knew what I was doing.

10. After a lot of persuading, our parents (**repressed, concurred**) in our plans to make a bicycle tour of New England.

11. Why should he be so talkative about most things but so (**voluble, reticent**) about his own personal background?

12. For centuries scholars have argued over how to (**explicate, renounce**) certain cryptic passages in Shakespeare.

13. Lacking a positive program of his own, he hoped to gain the support of the voters by (**concurring, defaming**) the other candidates.

14. With deep (**pandemonium, chagrin**), I must confess that I was the one who neglected to hire the orchestra for the class dance.

15. Will I ever again sleep as deeply as I did on those deliciously (**somnolent, raucous**) afternoons on that hot, quiet beach!

16. In unforgettable words, the prophet Micah called on men to (**acclimate, renounce**) the use of armed force.

17. The figures in the surrealistic painting had the (**grotesque, reticent**) appearance of characters in a nightmare.

18. I was startled not so much by his disapproval of my proposal as by the (**chagrin, vehemence**) with which he denounced it.

19. While the rest of us struggled with the math problem, Meg's (**receptive, complacent**) smirk as much as announced that she had already solved it.

20. Without work to challenge his ability and give him a sense of purpose, he felt that life had lost its (**savor, somnolence**).

Analogies   *In each of the following, encircle the item that best completes the comparison.*

1. **savory** is to **taste** as
   a. abrasive is to sight
   b. raucous is to sound
   c. exuberant is to odor
   d. patent is to texture

2. **jubilant** is to **chagrin** as
   a. phlegmatic is to alacrity
   b. magnanimous is to liberality
   c. sedate is to decorum
   d. vivacious is to liveliness

3. **somnolent** is to **doze** as
   a. vivacious is to militate
   b. implacable is to rescind
   c. reticent is to divulge
   d. indolent is to loll

4. **receptive** is to **take in** as
   a. sedate is to wake up
   b. mandatory is to wipe out
   c. dissonant is to smooth out
   d. abrasive is to wear down

5. **small** is to **infinitesimal** as
   a. large is to innocuous
   b. fat is to voluble
   c. big is to gigantic
   d. wide is to vehement

6. **patent** is to **invention** as
   a. trademark is to brand
   b. license is to vehicle
   c. copyright is to book
   d. title is to name

7. **complacent** is to **disgruntled** as
   a. zealous is to indifferent
   b. stentorian is to raucous
   c. mandatory is to vehement
   d. receptive is to retentive

8. **magnanimous** is to **favorable** as
   a. raucous is to unfavorable
   b. nondescript is to favorable
   c. vivacious is to unfavorable
   d. grotesque is to favorable

9. **elucidate** is to **clearer** as
   a. stipulate is to newer
   b. alleviate is to milder
   c. acclimate is to stranger
   d. rescind is to stronger

10. **asset** is to **liability** as
    a. apple is to orange
    b. north is to east
    c. plus is to minus
    d. black is to green

11. **abdicate** is to **throne** as
    a. stipulate is to condition
    b. deliver is to ultimatum
    c. enforce is to edict
    d. renounce is to title

12. **facsimile** is to **same** as
    a. prowess is to opposite
    b. antipathy is to same
    c. antithesis is to opposite
    d. ultimatum is to same

13. **zeal** is to **fervent** as
    a. prowess is to valorous
    b. chagrin is to exuberant
    c. compassion is to reticent
    d. magnanimity is to stentorian

14. **vivacious** is to **phlegmatic** as
    a. hearty is to merry
    b. carefree is to careless
    c. vehement is to grotesque
    d. jaunty is to morose

15. **bellicose** is to **threaten** as
    a. nondescript is to whet
    b. droll is to amuse
    c. innocuous is to appall
    d. grotesque is to comfort

16. **voluble** is to **much** as
    a. loquacious is to little
    b. complacent is to much
    c. reticent is to little
    d. infinitesimal is to much

17. **silence** is to **pandemonium** as
    a. dignity is to decorum
    b. order is to anarchy
    c. quarrel is to fracas
    d. force is to duress

18. **stimulate** is to **interest** as
    a. repress is to laughter
    b. whet is to appetite
    c. beset is to pleasure
    d. imbibe is to mouth

R

Identification *In each of the following groups, encircle the word that is best defined or suggested by the introductory phrase.*

1. an official proclamation with the force of law
a. droll b. chagrin c. edict d. grotesque

2. a salesman known for his fast, smooth talk
a. reticent b. voluble c. abrasive d. phlegmatic

3. This is my final offer—take it or leave it!
a. asset b. ultimatum c. antithesis d. savory

4. grounds for a lawsuit
a. prowess b. defamation c. ultimatum d. edict

5. a child who listens carefully and learns readily
a. sedate b. implacable c. nondescript d. receptive

6. a fight on the field soon broken up by the officials
a. alacrity b. decorum c. patent d. fracas

7. the world's greatest high jumper
a. chagrin b. prowess c. defamation d. antipathy

8. getting adjusted to a new job
a. sedated b. acclimated c. disparaged d. whetted

9. to include as a special point in a contract
a. imbibe b. stipulate c. laud d. renounce

10. I was never so embarrassed in my life.
a. chagrined b. reticent c. raucous d. zealous

11. "I do not like you, Dr. Fell. The reason why I cannot tell."
a. antipathy b. ultimatum c. antithesis d. edict

12. what one might try to do with a yawn
a. rescind b. sedate c. whet d. repress

13. accept an offer with cheerful promptness
a. alacrity b. decorum c. duress d. defamation

14. Please explain what you meant by those remarks!
a. alleviate b. rescind c. elucidate d. acclimate

15. spent the entire afternoon in the hammock
a. rescind b. loll c. beset d. stipulate

16. sympathy for those less fortunate than ourselves
a. compassion b. facsimile c. decorum d. antithesis

17. the exact opposite of what was expected
a. alacrity b. antithesis c. decorum d. facsimile

18. children at a party running about in wild disorder
a. chagrin b. savory c. edict d. pandemonium

19. overcome with shock and dismay
a. appalled b. whetted c. stipulated d. beset

20. like the cat that swallowed the canary
a. complacent b. droll c. savory d. grotesque

Shades of Meaning

Read each sentence carefully. Then encircle the item that best completes the statement below the sentence.

I was interested to learn that my lawyer friend specialized in patent law and made a handsome income from it. **(2)**

1. The word **patent** in line 1 most nearly means
   a. common   b. copyright   c. obvious   d. church

Before working on a tooth, a dentist will usually sedate the target area with some kind of local anesthetic. **(2)**

2. In line 1 the word **sedate** is used to mean
   a. sober   b. isolate   c. quiet   d. numb

When viewed from below, the lofty peaks that beset the little village in the valley seem to touch the very gates of heaven. **(2)**

3. The word **beset** in line 1 is best defined as
   a. surround   b. worry   c. stud   d. harass

Nary a ripple disturbed the tranquil surface of our phlegmatic little brook on that lazy summer afternoon. **(2)**

4. The word **phlegmatic** in line 1 most nearly means
   a. sluggish   b. impassive   c. muddy   d. unemotional

"Love, schmov!" I said. "One could hardly expect such a principled woman to marry a man whose past was scarcely savory." **(2)**

5. In line 2 the word **savory** most nearly means
   a. pungent   b. shady   c. respectable   d. enjoyable

Antonyms

*In each of the following groups, encircle the word or expression that is most nearly the **opposite** of the first word in **boldface type**.*

1. **mandatory**
   a. optional
   b. greedy
   c. silent
   d. needed

2. **imbibe**
   a. eject
   b. hurt
   c. help
   d. praise

3. **laud**
   a. appall
   b. elucidate
   c. disparage
   d. beset

4. **innocuous**
   a. kind
   b. harmful
   c. necessary
   d. open

5. **savory**
   a. ugly
   b. distasteful
   c. settled
   d. costly

6. **facsimile**
   a. speed
   b. difficulty
   c. original
   d. cruelty

7. **asset**
   a. dislike
   b. disagreement
   c. ability
   d. disadvantage

8. **abrasive**
   a. discouraging
   b. hard
   c. forceful
   d. soothing

9. implacable
a. severe
b. flexible
c. laughable
d. poor

12. concur
a. join
b. bring
c. disagree
d. please

15. phlegmatic
a. strong
b. strange
c. lively
d. amusing

18. stipulate
a. demand
b. take
c. agree
d. renounce

10. stentorian
a. repeated
b. tiny
c. seated
d. hushed

13. raucous
a. small
b. mellow
c. dangerous
d. safe

16. defamation
a. praise
b. advantage
c. pity
d. agreement

19. reticent
a. grotesque
b. receptive
c. voluble
d. applicable

11. magnanimous
a. sleepy
b. mean
c. slow
d. eager

14. nondescript
a. funny
b. lively
c. distinctive
d. confusing

17. droll
a. loud
b. large
c. funny
d. grim

20. vehement
a. strong
b. weak
c. messy
d. convincing

Completing the Sentence

From the following list of words, choose the one that best completes each of the sentences below. Write the word in the appropriate space.

Group A

imbibe	**whet**	**antipathy**	**prowess**
applicable	**decorum**	**chagrin**	**pandemonium**
repress	**receptive**	**alacrity**	**rescind**

1. The long wait in line to get into the stadium only _____ our appetite to see the big game.

2. We cannot _____ helpful traffic regulations simply because some drivers don't like them.

3. I think that we should make an effort to behave with more _____ during the assembly period.

4. The statistics you have cited may be accurate, but in my opinion they are not _____ to the problem facing us now.

5. Her _____ as a figure skater has made her both rich and famous.

Group B

implacable	**asset**	**appall**	**savory**
antithesis	**facsimile**	**stentorian**	**elucidate**
somnolent	**ultimatum**	**mandatory**	**laud**

1. The candidate's ability to speak effectively to all kinds of audiences proved an invaluable _____ during the long campaign.

2. The two brothers look much alike, but in personality and character each is the _____ of the other.

3. The night was punctuated by the _____ boom of the heavy artillery.

4. My Uncle Morris didn't just offer advice or make requests; he delivered a(n) _____ that he expected to be obeyed.

5. We were trying hard to be alert, but the heavy food, the warm room, and the drone of his voice quickly put us into a(n) _____ state.

Word Families

A. *On the line provided, write a* **noun form** *of each of the following words.*

EXAMPLE: zealous — **zeal**

1. stipulate _____
2. exuberant _____
3. renounce _____
4. disparage _____
5. magnanimous _____
6. receptive _____
7. alleviate _____
8. abrasive _____
9. grotesque _____
10. reticent _____
11. elucidate _____
12. acclimate _____
13. concur _____
14. explicate _____
15. repress _____
16. sedate _____
17. bellicose _____
18. dissonant _____
19. loquacious _____

B. *On the line provided, write a* **verb** *related to each of the following words.*

EXAMPLE: defamation — **defame**

1. savory _____
2. applicable _____
3. receptive _____
4. abrasive _____
5. mandatory _____

Filling the Blanks

Encircle the pair of words that best complete the meaning of each of the following passages.

1. I might not be so _____ about suggesting improvements at the office if my boss were more _____ to constructive criticism. But since he seems to resent it, I keep such ideas to myself.
   a. phlegmatic . . . implacable
   b. zealous . . . magnanimous
   c. reticent . . . receptive
   d. exuberant . . . compassionate

2. Though the supply of winter uniforms had done much to _____ the hardship suffered by the troops, the continuing shortage of ammunition and the ominous weather forecast _____ against pressing the attack.
   a. beset . . . concurred
   b. alleviate . . . militated
   c. acclimate . . . stipulated
   d. whet . . . elucidated

3. Though it didn't rule out mild soap, the warranty expressly _____ that _____ cleansers should not be used on the floor, since they would damage the tile surface.
   a. stipulated . . . abrasive
   b. explicated . . . innocuous
   c. rescinded . . . applicable
   d. concurred . . . dissonant

4. Alexander the Great was a(n) _____ foe of the Persians as long as they posed a threat to Greek security. But once he had conquered them, he proved to be a(n) _____ and even-handed ruler.
   a. vehement . . . repressive
   b. somnolent . . . innocuous
   c. phlegmatic . . . nondescript
   d. implacable . . . magnanimous

5. "Since the documents are only _____ of the Declaration of Independence," the salesperson said, "the price I'm asking for them is _____ in comparison to what the real thing would cost."
   a. antitheses . . . grotesque
   b. facsimiles . . . infinitesimal
   c. patents . . . colossal
   d. edicts . . . voluble

6. Like a Roman emperor of old, the new principal issued a(n) _____ stating that attendance at morning assembly, which had been optional under the old regime, was now _____ .
   a. edict . . . mandatory
   b. facsimile . . . applicable
   c. patent . . . complacent
   d. defamation . . . sedate

7. Edna's _____ , offbeat sense of humor proved to be a considerable _____ in the competition for class wit.
   a. nondescript . . . facsimile
   b. grotesque . . . antithesis
   c. savory . . . fracas
   d. droll . . . asset

Analogies   *In each of the following, encircle the item that best completes the comparison.*

1. **laggard** is to **alacrity** as
a. renegade is to duplicity
b. martinet is to discipline
c. bully is to belligerence
d. craven is to valor

2. **zealous** is to **apathy** as
a. ardent is to enthusiasm
b. sophomoric is to maturity
c. brash is to temerity
d. omniscient is to knowledge

3. **antipathy** is to **abhor** as
a. loathing is to laud
b. fondness is to relish
c. dislike is to esteem
d. partiality is to appall

4. **claim** is to **renounce** as
a. sword is to brandish
b. indemnity is to recompense
c. wrong is to redress
d. right is to waive

5. **innocuous** is to **virulent** as
a. placid is to turbulent
b. receptive is to amenable
c. disheveled is to unkempt
d. dour is to obnoxious

6. **garrulous** is to **loquacious** as
a. sedate is to vivacious
b. parsimonious is to magnanimous
c. scrupulous is to meticulous
d. nocturnal is to culinary

7. **implacable** is to **clemency** as
a. clairvoyant is to sensitivity
b. ingenuous is to guile
c. chivalrous is to magnanimity
d. stolid is to integrity

8. **complacent** is to **smug** as
a. explicit is to tacit
b. urbane is to suave
c. decrepit is to obsolete
d. endemic is to negligible

9. **abrasive** is to **erode** as
a. conclusive is to flood
b. coercive is to plunder
c. tentative is to demolish
d. corrosive is to burn

10. **pungent** is to **smell** as
a. musty is to touch
b. gnarled is to hearing
c. savory is to taste
d. fallow is to sight

11. **crestfallen** is to **chagrin** as
a. elated is to exhilaration
b. complacent is to apprehension
c. blithe is to dismay
d. somber is to compunction

12. **speech** is to **voluble** as
a. food is to palatable
b. income is to multifarious
c. writing is to voluminous
d. thought is to spontaneous

13. **contentious** is to **bellicose** as
a. mandatory is to optional
b. recalcitrant is to receptive
c. squalid is to opulent
d. truculent is to belligerent

14. **chaos** is to **turbulent** as
a. conflagration is to dissonant
b. pandemonium is to raucous
c. holocaust is to sonorous
d. fracas is to quiescent

15. **vehement** is to **energy** as
a. potent is to edge
b. cogent is to force
c. trenchant is to clout
d. acrid is to insight

16. **gibes** are to **disparage** as
a. platitudes are to deride
b. jeers are to commend
c. condolences are to defame
d. compliments are to extol

17. **malevolent** is to **rancor** as
a. phlegmatic is to torpor
b. stolid is to animosity
c. nonchalant is to concern
d. impervious is to receptivity

18. **applicable** is to **irrelevant** as
a. capricious is to inconstant
b. doting is to indulgent
c. kindred is to incompatible
d. copious is to inanimate

19. poignant is to **touch** as
a. limpid is to stroke
b. droll is to tickle
c. ironic is to brush
d. ominous is to rub

20. order is to **rescind** as
a. belief is to abjure
b. reference is to allude
c. agreement is to concur
d. problem is to explicate

21. grave is to **interment** as
a. shelf is to scrutiny
b. buffet is to consecrate
c. bed is to repose
d. chair is to sojourn

22. perceptible is to **discern** as
a. pliable is to stiffen
b. virulent is to control
c. indelible is to expunge
d. feasible is to do

Shades of Meaning   *Read each sentence carefully. Then encircle the item that best completes the statement below the sentence.*

Suddenly the clouds broke, the sun came out, and the whole garden was filled with the suave scent of lilacs.   (2)

1. In line 2 the word **suave** most nearly means
a. agreeable   b. sharp   c. urbane   d. polite

Beset with fewer precious stones, Monomakh's coronation cap is much easier to wear than Catherine's jewel-encrusted crown.   (2)

2. In line 1 the word **Beset** is used to mean
a. Hemmed in   b. Bedeviled   c. Harassed   d. Studded

Brave is the actress who would take on Scarlett O'Hara after Vivien Leigh's indelible screen performance of the role.   (2)

3. The word **indelible** in line 2 most nearly means
a. permanent   b. recent   c. unforgettable   d. sensitive

"Since a dull blade is likely to cause an accident," the chef advised, "always whet your knives before you use them."   (2)

4. The word **whet** in line 2 is used to mean
a. excite   b. stimulate   c. hone   d. prepare

As the fatigues of the day slowly overwhelmed me and sleep set in, my head began to loll lower and lower on my chest.   (2)

5. In line 2 the word **loll** can be defined as
a. loaf   b. droop   c. lounge   d. loiter

"Then the people cried out to their captains
For there was dearth in the land of their fathers,   (2)
'Let us hie to the valley of Glubdub,
Where the honey is sweet and will feed us.' "   (4)
      (A.E. Glug, *The Clodyssey*, III, 127–30)

6. The word **dearth** in line 2 most nearly means
a. austerity   b. depression   c. war   d. famine

124

**Filling
the Blanks**

*Encircle the pair of words that best complete the
meaning of each of the following passages.*

1. Although I'd been wide-awake when I'd entered the auditorium, the
_____ effect of the speaker's droning voice and tired
platitudes was so _____ that I began to fall asleep.
   a. uncanny . . . infinitesimal   c. somnolent . . . stultifying
   b. lamentable . . . negligible   d. averse . . . exhilarating

2. The leering faces of _____ gargoyles and other bizarre
monsters _____ from the walls, towers, and battlements of
medieval churches and castles like so many fantastic hunting trophies
hung over a fireplace.
   a. blithe . . . ruminate   c. garrulous . . . gape
   b. grotesque . . . protrude   d. supercilious . . . skulk

3. The _____ little "difference of opinion" suddenly developed
into an ugly _____ when the two people involved in the
dispute started throwing punches at each other.
   a. nondescript . . . antithesis   c. insidious . . . quandary
   b. squalid . . . scrutiny   d. amicable . . . fracas

4. When the Montagues and their _____ , the Capulets,
decided to settle their feud in the streets of Verona, the authorities had to
be called in to _____ the riot that ensued.
   a. adversaries . . . quell   c. renegades . . . repress
   b. martinets . . . chastise   d. exponents . . . suppress

5. When the weather's fine, I enjoy _____ on the beach, but
when it's _____ , I prefer to bask under a sunlamp.
   a. sojourning . . . infallible   c. embarking . . . capricious
   b. reposing . . . palatable   d. lolling . . . inclement

6. Though _____ invariably squander their _____
in no time at all, frugal people may often amass comfortable "nest eggs"
over the years.
   a. deviates . . . precedents   c. wastrels . . . assets
   b. benefactors . . . attainments   d. clairvoyants . . . itineraries

7. The account he gave of his actions on that fateful night was so full of
_____ and inconsistencies that I did not think it would be
_____ for him to convince a jury of his innocence.
   a. discrepancies . . . feasible   c. precedents . . . cogent
   b. panaceas . . . facile   d. gibes . . . scrupulous

8. Recognizing that an enemy assault on the right would put his entire battle formation in _____ , the commander ordered his reserve troops _____ to reinforce the exposed flank.

    a. demise . . . augmented   c. holocaust . . . coerced
    b. jeopardy . . . deployed   c. duplicity . . . retrogressed

9. The author was gratified by the lavish praise offered by the many critics who _____ her new novel, but she was perplexed and disappointed by the _____ welcome the book received from the public.

    a. extolled . . . tepid   c. reiterated . . . insidious
    b. scrutinized . . . benevolent   d. deleted . . . dour

10. The suspect had been observed _____ furtively in an alleyway an hour before the assault occurred, which suggests that a _____ crime rather than a chance mishap was involved.

    a. skulking . . . premeditated   c. plodding . . . truculent
    b. reposing . . . finite   d. brandishing . . . malevolent

11. The military governor began to grow _____ when the brutal _____ he ordered against the populace for acts of sabotage failed to curb their spirit of resistance.

    a. recalcitrant . . . condolences   c. corrosive . . . quandaries
    b. apprehensive . . . reprisals   d. assiduous . . . indemnities

12. In Pennsylvania's Amish country a visitor can still see _____ a way of life that elsewhere in this vast country has long since become _____ .

    a. copious . . . decrepit   c. extant . . . obsolete
    b. multifarious . . . emaciated   d. limpid . . . poignant

13. Copernicus, Galileo, and other _____ of the sun-centered theory of the our galaxy were in the _____ of the "scientific revolution" that has ultimately led to human beings walking on the moon.

    a. misnomers . . . plagiarism   c. wastrels . . . conflagration
    b. clairvoyants . . . retribution   d. exponents . . . vanguard

14. After our upset defeat we realized, to our _____ , that our early string of easy victories had turned us _____ and dulled our competitive edge.

    a. prowess . . . implacable   c. chagrin . . . complacent
    b. duress . . . receptive   d. alacrity . . . stentorian

Final Mastery Test

I. Selecting Word Meanings

*In each of the following groups, encircle the word or expression that is most nearly **the same** in meaning as the word in **boldface type** in the introductory phrase.*

1. test of **fortitude**
a. skill
b. courage
c. conscience
d. intelligence

2. augment his income
a. insure
b. increase
c. spend
d. waste

3. an **opulent** lifestyle
a. luxurious
b. dull
c. boring
d. poverty-stricken

4. reiterate an opinion
a. express
b. attack
c. defend
d. repeat

5. averse to strenuous exercise
a. opposed
b. accustomed
c. devoted
d. untrained

6. a **bellicose** personality
a. complacent
b. boring
c. quarrelsome
d. kindly

7. place in **jeopardy**
a. jail
b. custody
c. danger
d. safety

8. become a **culinary** expert
a. world
b. cooking
c. music
d. travel

9. time to **muse**
a. entertain
b. ponder
c. relax
d. study

10. harass the driver
a. help
b. accompany
c. annoy
d. dismiss

11. a **malevolent** attitude
a. spiteful
b. protective
c. indifferent
d. loving

12. an **invulnerable** position
a. safe
b. dangerous
c. isolated
d. important

13. unfeigned interest
a. businesslike
b. private
c. sincere
d. hypocritical

14. an **omniscient** deity
a. hardworking
b. veteran
c. all-knowing
d. conscientious

15. remiss in her work
a. excellent
b. skilled
c. scrupulous
d. careless

16. an **infallible** method
a. foolproof
b. scientific
c. fallacious
d. unproved

17. a **diffident** visitor
a. unexpected
b. shy
c. rude
d. welcome

18. an **inopportune** time
a. early
b. late
c. inconvenient
d. pleasant

19. guilty of **duplicity**
a. murder
b. bad taste
c. stubbornness
d. deceitfulness

20. his **ominous** appearance
a. threatening
b. impressive
c. attractive
d. unexplained

21. **vociferous** protests
a. frequent   b. subtle   c. noisy   d. reasonable

22. a **commodious** harbor
a. distant   b. well-run   c. costly   d. roomy

23. **voluminous** correspondence
a. confidential   b. abundant   c. infrequent   d. official

24. **squalid** conditions
a. healthful   b. exacting   c. ideal   d. wretched

25. **apprehensive** feelings
a. worried   b. elated   c. indescribable   d. unreasonable

II. Antonyms   In each of the following groups, encircle the **two** words or expressions that are most nearly **opposite** in meaning.

26. a. commend   b. consecrate   c. criticize   d. sacrifice
27. a. enthusiastic   b. agreeable   c. contentious   d. attentive
28. a. weak   b. potent   c. illegal   d. beneficial
29. a. confirm   b. attain   c. arouse   d. rescind
30. a. youthful   b. expected   c. dour   d. amicable
31. a. scrupulous   b. glorious   c. natural   d. cursory
32. a. incite   b. organize   c. train   d. quell
33. a. intellectual   b. petty   c. magnanimous   d. disturbed
34. a. palatable   b. dangerous   c. disagreeable   d. foolish
35. a. wealthy   b. scientific   c. assiduous   d. lazy
36. a. obey   b. antagonize   c. placate   d. remain
37. a. infinitesimal   b. loquacious   c. colossal   d. profitable
38. a. deny   b. embezzle   c. clarify   d. profess
39. a. foreign   b. disheveled   c. well-groomed   d. charming
40. a. asset   b. unwillingness   c. allure   d. alacrity

III. Supplying Words in Context   In each of the sentences below, write in the blank space the most appropriate word chosen from the following list.

Group A

abhor	vehement	esteem	suave
solace	consecrate	conclusive	trenchant
gibe	sedate	vivacious	suppress
temerity	guile	warily	somber

41. I find some _____ for our failure in the knowledge that we did everything we possibly could.

42. Her _____ remarks cut right to the heart of the issue under discussion.

43. The fingerprints were regarded as _____ evidence of his guilt.

44. Her _____ personality did much to enliven the party.

45. How does he have the _____ to criticize people who have done so much for him?

46. The dismal winter landscape put him in a very _____ mood.

47. Let's ignore their vicious _____ and do what we think is right.

48. He is so _____ that he seems to fit into any social situation without the slightest difficulty.

49. The dictator was unable to _____ the spirit of freedom.

50. We _____ racism, but we feel pity rather than hate for the racists.

Group B

adversary	ironic	implicate	altruistic
insidious	inveterate	condolence	dearth
multifarious	tacit	impervious	clairvoyant
misnomer	facsimile	feasible	redress

51. Isn't it _____ that he resigned from the editorship just before the newspaper received the award he had done so much to earn?

52. With all her _____ activities, it's a wonder that she finds time to sleep.

53. He is so sure of his own virtues that he is just about _____ to criticism.

54. As a(n) _____ concertgoer, he has seen many great musicians perform.

55. Janie's uncanny ability to guess what I'm thinking at any moment sometimes verges on the _____ .

56. Not a word was said, but there was a(n) _____ understanding that we would go to the dance together.

57. I'll have to be at my best to have a chance against a(n) _____ like Ken.

58. It would certainly be a(n) _____ to nickname that unscrupulous crook "Honest John."

59. The plan was deemed not _____ since there weren't sufficient funds to put it into effect.

60. Just when strong leadership is all-important, we find ourselves suffering from a(n) _____ of qualified leaders.

IV. Words Connected with Law and Government *The words in Column A may be applied to various situations connected with law and government. In the space before each word, write the **letter** of the item in Column B that identifies it.*

Column A	Column B
_____ **61.** abjure	a. a formal command by a governmental authority
_____ **62.** punitive	b. to change or add to a law
_____ **63.** ultimatum	c. based on the will of the people
_____ **64.** defamation	d. possessing unlimited power, as a dictator
_____ **65.** edict	e. to repudiate under oath
_____ **66.** precedent	f. relating to punishment
_____ **67.** amend	g. to pass on to one's heirs
_____ **68.** mandatory	h. unfair injury to a person's good name
_____ **69.** omnipotent	i. relating to law-making
_____ **70.** bequeath	j. a final demand by a government
	k. obligatory; required by law or regulation
	l. a judicial decision serving as a basis for later decisions

---

V. Words That Describe People *Some words that describe people are listed below. Write the appropriate word on the line next to each of the following descriptions.*

adroit	raucous	chivalrous	implacable
reprehensible	corrosive	august	indulgent
exuberant	meticulous	exemplary	sophomoric
nonchalant	stentorian	brash	officious

71. I admire the grace and courtesy with which Tom treated that elderly lady.

_____

72. She takes everything in stride and remains calm and unruffled in situations that would upset other people.

_____

73. When he feels that he has been wronged, he will never be satisfied until he "gets even."

_____

74. Ms. Heyland, our English teacher, encourages us to pay careful attention to every detail of grammar, usage, and punctuation.

_____

75. He is an outstanding citizen of this community who can well serve as a model for young people.

_____

76. She's always meddling in other people's affairs.

_____

77. I admire the cleverness and skill with which Amy handles people in situations in which others might be extremely awkward.

_____

78. Bob's foolish chatter and know-it-all attitude make him a total bore.

_____

79. He has betrayed his trust and should be condemned by all decent people.

_____

80. My aunt is so fond of her children that she lets them do almost anything they want.

_____

VI. Word Associations   *In each of the following, encircle the word or expression that best completes the meaning of the sentence or answers the question, with particular reference to the meaning of the word in **boldface type**.*

81. You would **extol** something that you find
 a. contentious
 b. commendable
 c. corrosive
 d. crestfallen

82. To **skulk** out of a room suggests
 a. haste
 b. happiness
 c. sneakiness
 d. listlessness

83. Which of the following suggests that a team is being **derided?**
 a. "We're number one!"
 b. "Go and get 'em!"
 c. "You guys are losers!"
 d. "Give us a break, umpire!"

84. If you **concur** in a decision, you
 a. agree with it
 b. consider it wrong
 c. are indifferent to it
 d. are not aware of it

85. To be **somnolent** implies a desire to
 a. eat
 b. exercise
 c. get out of town
 d. sleep

86. We may apply the word **stately** to
 a. a duchess and a sailing ship
 b. a robot and a computer
 c. a city and a state
 d. nostalgia and panacea

87. The word **demise** suggests that someone or something has
 a. won a prize
 b. failed an examination
 c. passed out of existence
 d. gained final approval

88. A movie that is exceptionally **poignant** is likely to
 a. put you to sleep
 b. touch your emotions
 c. get a lot of laughs
 d. fail at the box office

89. The word **holocaust** can be applied to
 a. a trivial event
 b. an amusing misunderstanding
 c. a long war that ends in a draw
 d. a historical tragedy costing many lives

90. A picture that is **askew** should be
a. dusted
b. given a price
c. straightened
d. sold to the highest bidder

91. You would criticize a **wastrel** for
a. being lazy
b. talking too loudly
c. squandering money
d. not telling the truth

92. Which nickname would a **parsimonious** person be most likely to have?
a. Alibi Ike
b. El Cheapo
c. Fancy Dan
d. Calamity Jane

93. Which of the following phrases suggests something that is **nondescript?**
a. something the cat dragged in
b. bright-eyed and bushy-tailed
c. cute as a button
d. ready for action

94. Which of the following might be called **innocuous?**
a. a neighborhood gossip
b. a devoted community worker
c. a religious leader
d. a well-meaning but ineffectual person

95. An expenditure of money is **negligible** when it is
a. illegal
b. too small to worry about
c. excessive
d. legal but not morally justified

96. A well-known **renegade** in American history is
a. Daniel Boone
b. Abigail Adams
c. Edgar Allan Poe
d. Benedict Arnold

97. If people refer to Dave as **unkempt,** he should try to
a. speak more clearly
b. improve his grooming
c. smile more often
d. learn to play bridge

98. You would be most likely to read of **uncanny** events in
a. a history textbook
b. a detective story
c. a novel of social protest
d. a ghost story

99. A nation that is a **belligerent** is engaged in
a. war
b. industrialization
c. land reform
d. energy conservation

100. Which of the following might be described as **lamentable?**
a. winning a scholarship
b. visiting a sick friend
c. getting a new car
d. failing to do well on this Final Test

Building with Word Roots

Units 1-3

mis, miss, mit, mitt—to send

This root appears in **demise** (page 20). The literal meaning is "a sending down," but the word now suggests a death, especially of a person in an elevated position. Some other words based on the same root are listed below.

commissary	**emit**	**manumit**	**premise**
emissary	**intermittently**	**missile**	**remission**

From the list of words above, choose the one that corresponds to each of the brief definitions below. Write the word on the line at the right of the definition, and then in the illustrative phrase below the definition.

1. to free from slavery or bondage   _____

_____ the indentured servants

2. a messenger, agent (*"one sent out"*)   _____

_____ chosen to negotiate a surrender

3. a place where supplies are distributed; a lunchroom   _____

buy provisions at the _____

4. coming and going at intervals; not continuously (*"sent between"*)   _____

 rained _____ during the night

5. an object to be thrown or shot   _____

fire a(n) _____ with deadly accuracy

6. a letup, abatement; a relief from suffering   _____

a brief _____ of the tempest

7. to release or send forth (*"send out"*)   _____

_____ a high-pitched warning signal

8. a statement or idea upon which a conclusion is based (*"that which is sent before"*)   _____

an argument based on a false _____

From the list of words above, choose the one that best completes each of the following sentences. Write the word in the space provided.

1. When he issued the Emancipation Proclamation in 1863, President Abraham Lincoln _____ four million enslaved human beings.

2. The families of the soldiers stationed on the base were able to buy food and clothing at the _____ .

3. The trapped rabbit _____ a frantic squeal and struggled in vain to escape the hawk's talons.

4. The Secretary of State went to the arms conference being held in a foreign capital as the official _____ of the United States.

5. It snowed _____ at first, stopping and starting a number of times before the steady downfall commenced.

6. The doctors had begun to give up hope when the disease suddenly went into _____ , and the patient began to recover.

7. In the hands of the old-time vaudeville comedian, a custard pie became a(n) _____ that could stop any pursuer in his or her tracks.

8. Basing his decision on the _____ that some child in the school was carrying an infectious disease, the doctor ordered all of the students to be inoculated.

Units 4-6

fac, fact—to make or do

This root appears in **facile,** "easily accomplished or done" (page 36). Some other words based on the same root are listed below.

artifact	**faction**	**factor**	**faculty**
facility	**factitious**	**factual**	**malefactor**

From the list of words above, choose the one that corresponds to each of the brief definitions below. Write the word on the line at the right of the definition, and then in the illustrative phrase below the definition.

1. based on fact, real _____

a(n) _____ report outlining just what had happened

2. ease, skill; that which serves or acts as a convenience or for a specific function _____

played the piano with great _____

3. a small group of people within a larger group _____

the _____ in favor of public ownership

4. one who commits a crime, evildoer (*"one who does evil"*) _____

arrested as a(n) _____

5. artificial, not natural; sham _____

_____ enthusiasm for the dictator

6. one of the elements that help to bring about a result; an agent _____

a major _____ in their success

7. an object of historical or archeological interest produced by human workmanship (*"something made with skill"*) _____

uncovered some Indian _____

8. a teaching staff; the ability to act or to do something _____

a(n) _____ for understanding people

From the list of words on page 133, choose the one that best completes each of the following sentences. Write the word in the space provided.

1. His major weakness, which keeps him from a position of leadership, is a complete lack of the _____ of self-criticism.

2. The speaker pointed out a number of ways in which we could raise the money necessary to increase the library _____ in our community.

3. The _____ of ancient cultures tell us a great deal about the day-to-day life of earlier civilizations.

4. What seems to be strong popular support for that program is in reality shallow and _____ .

5. What was once a united political party has been splintered into two or three warring _____ .

6. President Theodore Roosevelt criticized certain rich men as evildoers, calling them "_____ of great wealth."

7. Television has become a key _____ in determining public opinion and sharing popular tastes.

8. We are not dealing with opinions or interpretations but with a simple matter of _____ accuracy.

Units 7-9

voc, vok—to call

This root appears in **vociferous,** "loud or noisy" (page 55). Some other words based on the same root are listed below.

advocate	**convocation**	**evoke**	**revoke**
avocation	**equivocal**	**invoke**	**vocalize**

From the list of words above, choose the one that corresponds to each of the brief definitions below. Write the word on the line at the right of the definition, and then in the illustrative phrase below the definition.

1. to bring or call back; to annul by recalling _____

_____ a license to drive

2. to give voice to; to sing without words   _____

_____ one's fears

3. to plead in favor of; one who defends a course; one who pleads the cause of another   _____

_____ a revision of the proposal

4. open to two or more interpretations, ambiguous; uncertain or doubtful in nature   _____

a(n) _____ statement

5. a meeting, especially of members of a college or clergy ("a calling together")   _____

attend the _____

6. an occupation or activity pursued for enjoyment, in addition to one's regular work; a hobby   _____

a diverting _____

7. to call in for help or support; to appeal to as an authority; to put into effect; to make an earnest request for ("to call on")   _____

_____ their forgiveness

8. to call forth; bring to mind ("to call out")   _____

_____ a positive response

From the list of words on page 134, choose the one that best completes each of the following sentences. Write the word in the spaces provided.

1. A chemist by profession, Sarah has for many years pursued landscape painting as

a(n) _____ .

2. To warm up their voices, opera singers will _____ for a short time before going on the stage.

3. As if by magic, the actors on the bare stage _____ the sounds, shapes, and colors of a small New England town.

4. The new ordinance restricting bicycle traffic during rush hours proved to be so

unpopular that it was _____ .

5. To prevent the complete disruption of the city's transportation system, the governor

threatened to _____ the law that would send the union's leaders to jail for contempt.

6. The officer's _____ remarks suggested that he was of two minds about the enemy's will to resist.

7. The mayor has always _____ strict governmental regulation of building codes.

8. Dr. Elizabeth Mann is one of the specialists who have been invited to attend the

_____ of experts on problems in the health field.

Units 10-12

tac, tag, tang, teg, tet, ting—to touch

This root appears in **tangible,** "able to be seen or felt" (page 88). Some other words based on the same root are listed below.

contagious	**intangible**	**tact**	**tangent**
intact	**integral**	**tactile**	**tangential**

From the list of words above, choose the one that corresponds to each of the brief definitions below. Write the word on the line at the right of the definition, and then in the illustrative phrase below the definition.

1. unimpaired; whole, with no part missing   _____

    keep a collection _____

2. a keen sense of the right thing to say or do to avoid giving offense; diplomacy   _____

    show _____ in handling a delicate situation

3. essential for completeness; lacking nothing essential   _____

    a(n) _____ part of our organization

4. barely touching; only superficially relevant, digressive   _____

    a(n) _____ remark

5. capable of spreading from person to person, catching   _____

    a(n) _____ disease

6. of or relating to the sense of touch; perceptible to touch   _____

    a(n) _____ organ

7. not capable of being touched; not easily grasped by the mind   _____

    a(n) _____ asset

8. an abrupt change in course; touching at only one point   _____

    a straight line _____ to a curve

From the list of words above, choose the one that best completes each of the following sentences. Write the word in the space provided.

1. His remarks were so _____ to the subject of the discussion as to be practically beside the point.

2. If we want their support in the upcoming election, we must make their suggestions a(n) _____ part of our overall program.

3. What teacher has not discovered how _____ a yawn, sneeze, or cough can be in a classroom!

4. Modern technology has yet to produce an instrument or device that can match the consummate _____ sensitivity of a human finger.

5. None of the public buildings in the bombed city remained _____ after that most devastating air raid.

6. How can you describe something as _____ as a soul to one who has never before been exposed to the concept?

7. I am amazed that Alice, who is so blunt in talking to her friends, can show so much _____ when handling adults.

8. The speaker went off on a(n) _____ and never dealt directly with the topic under discussion.

Units 13-15

sed, sess, sid—to sit, settle

This root appears in **sedate** (page 102). The literal meaning is "settled," but the word now means "quiet or calm." Some other words based on the same root are listed below.

assess	**obsessed**	**sediment**	**subsidiary**
dissidence	**residual**	**subside**	**supersede**

From the list of words above, choose the one that corresponds to each of the brief definitions below. Write the word on the line at the right of the definition, and then in the illustrative phrase below the definition.

1. to displace in favor of another; replace; force out of use   _____

   _____ all the other officials

2. excessively troubled or preoccupied by   _____

   _____ by fear of illness

3. to grow less; become less active; to die down ("*to settle down*")   _____

   when the excitement _____

4. furnishing aid or support; of secondary importance; a thing or person that assists or supplements   _____

   a(n) _____ stream

5. matter that settles to the bottom of a liquid; lees, dregs   _____

   filtered out the _____

6. to estimate the value of; to fix an amount, tax; to determine the importance, value, or size of   _____

   _____ each member a dollar

7. disagreement in opinion or belief; dissent   _____

    a meeting marred by noisy _____

8. remaining; left over   _____

    _____ money

From the list of words on page 137, choose the one that best completes each of the following sentences. Write the word in the space provided.

1. Will nuclear fission ever _____ fossil fuels as the major source of energy in the United States?

2. The elderly are often _____ by the fear of being robbed or injured by young hoodlums.

3. Party officials sought to quell the growing _____ in the ranks by ousting the leaders of the disgruntled faction.

4. How accurately can present-day diagnostic tests _____ the true potential of any teenager?

5. When the floodwaters finally retreated, residents returned to find their little village covered with a layer of muddy _____ .

6. Under the United States Constitution, state governments may exercise those _____ powers which are not assigned to the Federal government and not forbidden to the states.

7. Only when the master of ceremonies finally raised his hand did the giggling in the audience _____ .

8. The raw materials needed by that giant corporation are supplied mainly by its own _____ companies.

The following tabulation lists all the basic words taught in the various units of this workbook, as well as those introduced in the *Vocabulary of Vocabulary* and *Building with Word Roots* sections. The number following each entry indicates the page on which the word is first introduced. Exercise and review materials in which the word also appears are not cited.